Acting Cool!

Using Reader's Theatre to Teach Language Arts and Social Studies in Your Classroom

By Chris Gustafson

LINWORTH LEARNING

From the Minds of Teachers

Linworth Publishing, Inc.
Worthington, Ohio

Library of Congress Cataloging-in-Publication Data

Gustafson, Chris, 1950-
    Reader's theater : language arts and social studies / by Chris Gustafson.
    p. cm.
    Includes bibliographical references.
    ISBN 1-58683-090-2 (pbk.)
    1. Drama in education. 2. Readers' theater. I. Title.
    PN3171.G89 2004
    371.39'9--dc21

                                            2003012886

Editor: Claire Morris
Design and Production: Good Neighbor Press, Inc., Grand Junction, Colorado 81503

Published by Linworth Publishing, Inc.
480 East Wilson Bridge Road, Suite L
Worthington, Ohio 43085

ISBN: 1-58683-090-2

5 4 3 2 1

Table of Contents

Table of Contents *(continued)*

National Standards for English and Language Arts

How to Use This Book

Reader's Theatre is a wonderful tool across the curriculum. Although specific topics taught at each grade level vary nationwide, national standards that promote excellence in most content areas do exist. Seeing a connection between national standards and a particular teaching unit is sometimes difficult. The plays in this book reinforce national standards by using situations that reflect best teaching practices and are fun for students. They are intended for use by middle school students, though some may be appropriate for lower or higher grades.

Each play comes with vocabulary, before reading, and after reading activities, many with grading standards. Use your own creativity and knowledge of your class to alter, omit, or add to these activities.

A bit of extra time will be needed the first time you use a play. Begin by asking if any students know what Reader's Theatre is. Only a couple of my students had any idea what was involved at the beginning of the year, so be sure students understand that Reader's Theatre is like doing a very short play, but no parts are memorized. Go over the following expectations for the performers.

- Skim over your parts to make sure you can pronounce all the words. Ask for help if there are words you don't know.

- Speak loudly enough so that you can be heard at the back of the classroom.

- Communicate using expressive voices and faces. Sound effects are encouraged, too.

- When you are not reading, do not draw attention to yourself by your facial expressions, fidgeting, or making noises.

The grading standard is intended to help evaluate a Reader's Theatre performance and can be filled out by the teacher, the student, or both. It's also effective to have a class imagine the best possible Reader's Theatre performance and use their ideas to create their own grading standard. Evaluating the performance of the audience is easy. The job of the audience is to listen attentively during the performance and clap politely after it is done.

Even if you don't use the vocabulary activities, there are probably some words in the piece that not everyone will know. They are listed before each script in this book. Depending on the reading level of the students you are working with, you may need to talk about what the words mean and how to pronounce them. You can add words, omit words, or skip this pre-teaching altogether, depending on your class.

There is a list of the characters before each script, with brief character descriptions. These should help students convey their characters since they won't have had time for more than a brief look at their part. After you've described the parts, ask for volunteers, but make it clear that you will assign parts if necessary.

If you are using a script that introduces a piece of literature or a historical character, it's helpful to give a brief introduction to the time period, the setting, and possibly the characters in the book. Some ideas for this summary are included before each literature script. A good time to do this is after you've handed out the scripts and while the actors are glancing over their parts, which are highlighted on each of the separate scripts, to make sure they can understand the words they're going to read.

When it is time for the play to begin, students stand in a line facing the audience. Ask them to say their character's name before they begin reading the script. This helps the audience to remember which student is reading the part of which character. It also helps the actors get a sense of how loudly they will have to read to be heard. It's an easy time to ask individuals to read more loudly. You can ask the actors to group themselves in a way that shows how their characters are related to each other. When they're ready, the reading begins.

Reader's Theatre works with regular education students, highly capable students, English language learners, fluent readers, average readers, and even those for whom reading is challenging. The occasional group comes in thinking they are "too cool" to perform; but once they have done it, most are anxious to do it again. ***Enjoy using these plays with your class!***

Name _____ Period _____ Date _____

Grading Standard for Performance

1. I used my voice and my facial expressions to make my reading interesting.

   1   **2**   **3**   **4**   **5**
   gave new meaning   lively and
   to "monotone"   interesting

2. I stood quietly when it wasn't my turn to read.

   1   **2**   **3**   **4**   **5**
   poked my   stood quietly
   neighbor

3. I read clearly and fluently.

   1   **2**   **3**   **4**   **5**
   forgot what quite a   read clearly
   few words sound like

4. My voice could be heard by the people in the back of the room.

   1   **2**   **3**   **4**   **5**
   they fell asleep   they heard me
   from boredom

5. I did my best and I'm proud of my performance.

   1   **2**   **3**   **4**   **5**
   blew it off   made myself
                                                                         proud

Total points _____

1

 # Social Studies Standards

1. Culture

2. Time, Continuity, and Change

3. People, Places, and Environments

4. Individual Development and Identity

5. Individuals, Groups, and Institutions

6. Power, Authority, and Governance

7. Production, Distribution, and Consumption

8. Science, Technology, and Society

9. Global Connections

10. Civic Ideals and Practices

Reprinted with permission from *Expectations of Excellence: Curriculum Standards for Social Studies by National Council for the Social Studies Staff*, Copyright ©1994 by National Council for the Social Studies.

A Teenager in Albania

by Chris Gustafson
NCSS 1, Culture

Vocabulary Activity

Give teams or groups of students the vocabulary page. Have them predict how the words would be used in a Reader's Theatre play titled *A Teenager in Albania*. Call on several groups to share their ideas, and discuss concepts about which they may be unsure.

Vocabulary Words

Albania—a small, Eastern European country

culture—characteristic aspects of the lives of a group of people

gjinar—a time after dinner when Albanian people meet and walk in the town square

pyramid scheme—an investment scheme in which people are lured into "investing" or sending money to participants at the top of a list with the promise that as more and more people join, they will eventually receive money themselves.

supervise—keep track of

Before Reading

Ask your class to imagine that they have been contacted by a school in Albania. The Albanian teens want to know what life is like for teenagers in the United States and are looking for pen pals. They're curious about chores, how students spend free time, allowances, what students like to buy, and what they do with their families. Have students write back to this imaginary Albanian class, describing their own lives in these areas.

Perform *A Teenager in Albania*

Cast of Characters

Narrator 1
Narrator 2
Jack's Mom—fairly calm, helpful, wry sense of humor
Jack—smart, hard-working

After Reading

Imagine that the Albanian pen pals have come to visit your students. What would the pen pals experience during their first week in the United States as they stay with your students and go to school? Have students write a journal entry from the point of view of the visiting Albanian student.

Culturegrams, *Albania*. Millenial Star Network and Brigham Young University, 2001.

Name _____ Period _____ _____ Date _____

Vocabulary Predictions

You are going to read a play called *A Teenager in Albania* that contains the following words. What do you predict the play will be about?

Vocabulary Words

Albania
culture
gjinar—a time after dinner when Albanian people meet and walk in the town square

pyramid scheme
supervise

First Prediction:

_____

_____

Second Prediction:

_____

_____

- -

Name _____ Period _____ Date _____

Vocabulary Predictions

You are going to read a play called *A Teenager in Albania* that contains the following words. What do you predict the play will be about?

Vocabulary Words

Albania
culture
gjinar—a time after dinner when Albanian people meet and walk in the town square

pyramid scheme
supervise

First Prediction:

_____

_____

Second Prediction:

_____

_____

A Letter to an Albanian Pen Pal

You have been contacted by a school in Albania. The Albanian teens want to know what life is like for teenagers in the United States and are looking for pen pals. They're curious about chores, how you spend free time, allowances, what you like to buy, and what you do with your family. Write back to your pen pal below, answering his/her questions.

_____

_____

_____

_____

_____

_____

_____

_____

_____

_____

_____

_____

_____

_____

A Teenager in Albania

by Chris Gustafson
NCSS 1, Culture

Jack's Mom: Jack, hurry up if you want me to listen to your oral report. I've got yoga tonight.

Jack: Just a minute, Mom.

Narrator 1: Jack picked up a stack of notecards.

Narrator 2: He found his Mom sitting at the kitchen table with a cup of tea.

Jack: Okay, I'm ready.

Jack's Mom: Go ahead and start.

Narrator 1: Jack began.

Jack: If I was a teenager in Albania.

Jack's Mom: Just a second. What's your report about?

Jack: What my life would be like if I was a teenager in Albania.

Jack's Mom: I thought this was your country report.

Jack: It is. I had to learn all about Albania. And I have to give an oral report on what it would be like to be a teenager there.

Jack's Mom: Oh, okay. Go ahead.

Jack: If I was a teenager in Albania, some parts of my life would be a lot different. Albania is a very poor country, but they're right on the edge of Europe. Just about everyone gets Italian radio and TV, so they see advertising and programs from much richer places. I'd never be able to afford a portable CD player, but I'd know lots of other kids my age have them.

Jack's Mom: I can imagine worse things in life. Some of the music you listen to!

Jack: Some things would be the same. I'd still play soccer with my friends. Every night after dinner there's this very cool time called "gjinar." I'm not sure how to pronounce it because I just read it in a book. Everyone in a neighborhood comes out to the town square and they walk around and talk with their friends. Sometimes there's dancing. It's a major hangout time for teens, and they see their friends and eat ice cream.

Jack's Mom: And their parents are around to supervise. That's good.

Jack: Mom!

Jack's Mom: I got some ice cream, by the way. Your favorite kind.

Jack: Thanks, Mom. Anyway, I probably wouldn't have a part-time job. Jobs are really scarce and money is tight. I'd have jobs to do around the house. The water is only on a couple of times a day. I'd hang around with some tubs to fill in case the water came on. Then there's the toilet paper trash.

Jack's Mom: Toilet paper trash?

Jack: Yeah. Most plumbing can't handle toilet paper so it never gets flushed, so someone has to collect it and . . .

Jack's Mom: Okay, okay. Your class doesn't need to know ALL the details.

Jack: That's the interesting part, Mom!

Narrator 1: Jack's mom sighed.

Jack's Mom: Go on.

Jack: This is the pretty sad part. Albania had a dictator for a long time, and after he was gone, the whole country went a little bit crazy. There was a pyramid scheme that almost everyone in the whole country got involved in. Do you know how those work?

Jack's Mom: Isn't that when you get some letter in the mail that says you should send a dollar to each person on a list? Then you add your name to the bottom of the list and take the name off the top of the list and send the letter on to six more people? Something hugely bad is supposed to happen to you if you break the chain.

Jack: Have you ever gotten one of those?

Jack's Mom: Oh, sure.

Jack: What did you do with it?

Jack's Mom: Threw it away.

Jack: The Albanian letters wanted a lot more than a dollar. It's like no one ever heard about pyramid schemes before so they all believed it would work. So many people were poor, and I guess it gave them hope that they could get rich quicker.

Jack's Mom: What happened?

Jack: It fell apart. Lots of people lost their homes because of it. I would probably live in a tiny apartment. Since I might have lived in a house before the pyramid scheme, the apartment would be all crammed with stuff we were hanging on to in case we could ever afford a bigger place.

Narrator 2: Jack's mom glanced at her watch.

Jack: I'm just about done. I would speak Albanian and Italian, but I would really want to learn English so I could leave Albania. I would be discouraged about my future because there really aren't any good jobs in Albania. I would study hard so I could go somewhere else and work. I'd probably have to send money home to help my family.

Jack's Mom: Send money to your family. Those Albanians have some very good ideas!

Jack: Mom! That's sad!

Jack's Mom: Yes, I guess it is. Good job, Jack. You learned a lot. I'm glad you're MY teen and not an Albanian teen.

Narrator 1: Jack's mom gave him a hug on her way out the door.

Narrator 2: Jack grinned. Then he opened the freezer and pulled out the chocolate chip mint ice cream.

Name _____ Period _____ Date _____

Journal Entry of an Albanian Teen

Imagine that the Albanian pen pals have come to visit. What would they experience during their first week in the United States, staying with you and going to your school? Write a journal entry from the point of view of the Albanian student staying with your family.

_____

_____

_____

_____

_____

_____

_____

_____

_____

_____

_____

_____

_____

_____

Name _____ Period _____ Date _____

 # Journal Entry Grading Standard

1. My journal entry includes at least three well-written paragraphs.

1   **2**   **3**   **4**   **5**

fewer, lame
paragraphs

at least three well-
written paragraphs

2. My paragraphs describe events at school and at home.

1   **2**   **3**   **4**   **5**

got stuck in one spot

both places

3. I read clearly and fluently.

1   **2**   **3**   **4**   **5**

not really

kept that
point of view

4. My voice could be heard by the people in the back of the room.

1   **2**   **3**   **4**   **5**

didn't do my best

my best work

Total points _____

- -

Name _____ Period _____ Date _____

 # Journal Entry Grading Standard

1. My journal entry includes at least three well-written paragraphs.

1   **2**   **3**   **4**   **5**

fewer, lame
paragraphs

at least three well-
written paragraphs

2. My paragraphs describe events at school and at home.

1   **2**   **3**   **4**   **5**

got stuck in one spot

both places

3. I read clearly and fluently.

1   **2**   **3**   **4**   **5**

not really

kept that
point of view

4. My voice could be heard by the people in the back of the room.

1   **2**   **3**   **4**   **5**

didn't do my best

my best work

Total points _____

Trench Warfare

by Chris Gustafson
NCSS 2, Time, Continuity, Change

Vocabulary Activity

Students will work individually or in groups to fill out the example/description/comparison chart of vocabulary words for this selection.

Vocabulary Words

barrage balloons—balloons supporting nets to deflect air attacks

elements—items

entries—short pieces of writing in a journal

mustard gas—a poison gas, heavier than air

wispy—thin, insubstantial

Zeppelin—German blimps

Before Reading

Students will work in groups using the graphic organizer to brainstorm what trench warfare is like. They will share their ideas with the rest of the class.

Perform *Trench Warfare*

Cast of Characters

Narrator 1
Narrator 2
Cal—excitable, doesn't like to read
Rasheed—keeps Cal on track
Mr. Wells—firm, clear

After Reading

Give students (individually or in teams) five minutes to create a model of trench warfare on their desktops, using only what they have in their desks, pockets, or binders. Have half the class take a gallery walk around the room, viewing the work of the other half of the class, who will explain the elements of their models to the gallery viewers. Then switch. Evaluate students on the number of elements they've included, or ask them to write a self-evaluation based on their effort and the elements included in their model.

Name _____ Period _____ Date _____

Trench Warfare Vocabulary

Fill in each box. Give an example of, description of, and comparison for, each word.

	Example	Description	Comparison
elements	The elements of fudge are milk, sugar, water, chocolate, and vanilla.	Parts of a whole	Elements are to something whole as chocolate chips are to chocolate chip cookies.
Zeppelin			
mustard gas			
wispy			
entries			
barrage balloons			

What Is Trench Warfare Like?

List ideas about what trench warfare is like inside the large circle. List the sources for your ideas outside the circle.

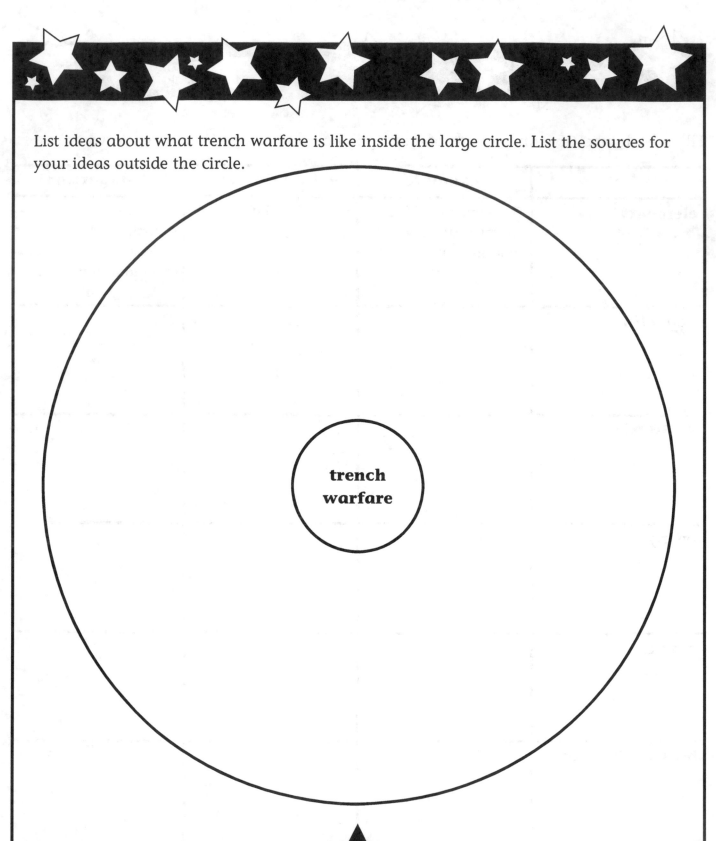

trench
warfare

Trench Warfare

by Chris Gustafson
NCSS 2, Time, Continuity, Change

Narrator 1: Cal made a face as Mr. Wells handed out the assignment sheet. It was time to start their final project on World War I.

Narrator 2: Cal wasn't crazy about writing reports. The last poster he'd made left his best friend Rasheed doubled over laughing. His teacher hadn't been too impressed, either.

Narrator 1: Cal was dreading the World War I project.

Mr. Wells: Okay, class, take a look at the assignment sheet.

Narrator 2: Cal started to read.

Cal: Rasheed, look. There's five things we have to do. I'll never get this done!

Narrator 1: Cal began to read down the list.

Cal: Pretend you're a soldier writing journal entries home from the front. Make a picture book teaching about World War I to third graders.

Rasheed: Calm down! You skipped the part at the top. It says "Choose one."

Narrator 2: Cal calmed down. He kept on reading.

Cal: Write a play about life in London during the Zeppelin raids.

Rasheed: Read the next one.

Cal: Build a model showing a typical battlefield on the western front. Include the following list of elements.

Rasheed: Soldiers for each side, trenches, tank traps. There's lots more. This looks really cool!

Mr. Wells: Just a reminder, everyone. You can't use anything purchased for any of the projects. Especially for the model—none of those little green soldiers that come in bags. No model tanks. You use it, you make it.

Narrator 1: Cal and Rasheed went over to Rasheed's house after school because his mom had a glue gun.

Cal: I heard Melissa and Marisol talking. They're going to make their model out of a chocolate sheet cake. All the props will be made out of candy.

Rasheed: That's so stupid. By the time it's due, it'll be crawling with mold.

Cal: That would look cool.

Rasheed: Ours will be way better. Let's see what we can find in the basement.

Narrator 1: Rasheed found a lot of cardboard, some wire, and construction paper.

Narrator 2: Cal used Rasheed's computer to find out what French and British uniforms looked like. He printed out old photos of tanks, flags, and a World War I airplane.

Rasheed: Super pictures! Did they use airplanes then?

Cal: It says that the first pilots were just scouts. They used to wave at the pilots in the enemy planes. But then they started dropping bricks and chains on each other. Pretty soon it was bombs, dogfights, and wing-mounted machine guns.

Narrator 1: Cal studied the photo and began to sketch the body of a plane on the cardboard.

Narrator 2: Cal and Rasheed worked on their project nearly every day after school.

Narrator 1: On the due date, they carefully set it on the counter in their classroom.

Mr. Wells: Take out your grading standards everyone, and do your self-evaluation. Then teams will present their projects.

Rasheed: We've got everything on our model!

Narrator 2: Rasheed and Cal carefully checked off the requirements on their grading standards.

Rasheed: Popsicle sticks make excellent tank traps.

Cal: I like the way you colored the cotton balls and pulled them apart. It looks wispy on the ground, just like mustard gas.

Narrator 1: Cal and Rasheed presented their project. Cal pointed out the pilot holding the brick in the French fighter plane. The plane dangled from a bent piece of wire coat hanger.

Narrator 2: Rasheed told about barrage balloons. He had made one out of part of a plastic glove.

Mr. Wells: Well done, you two.

Narrator 1: As they listened to the next student's presentation, Rasheed pulled out a napkin and handed it to Cal.

Narrator 2: Inside was a small, lumpy piece of chocolate cake.

Cal: What's that?

Rasheed: It's a piece of Melissa and Marisol's trench warfare model made out of chocolate cake. Marisol's dog bit off one corner before they left for school this morning. She broke this piece off to even it up.

Cal: She says!

Narrator 1: Rasheed looked suspiciously at the piece of cake.

Narrator 2: Then he shrugged and took a bite.

Mapping the State

by Chris Gustafson
NCSS 3, People, Places, Environments

Vocabulary Activity

As a class or in groups, have students complete the vocabulary definition page.

Vocabulary Words

atlas—a book containing maps

geography—the physical features of an area

scale—changing the size of something while keeping the proportions the same

Before Reading

As a class or in groups, fill out the "Parts of a Map" form. For each element students identify, brainstorm examples of sub-elements.

Perform Mapping the State

Cast of Characters

Narrator 1
Narrator 2
Thuy—annoyed
Clarice—pragmatic, sees the cup half full
John—kind of a flirt

After Reading

Integrate this play with what your students are learning in social studies. Have them make a theme map of a city, a region, or a country. In addition to the appropriate geographic elements, have students look for a common feature that is found in three to five places on their map. A paragraph describing the common feature in each area is typed and attached to the border of the map. Work with students to create a grading standard for this project before they begin the work.

Vocabulary Definitions for Mapping the State

Define each word by finding a category the word belongs to and listing characteristics of the word. The first one has been done as an example.

1. Scale is:	a way of showing size that	• has something small represent something large. • shows a mathematical relationship. • is used on maps.
2. Geography is:		
3. An atlas is:		

Parts of a Map

Map		
	1. outline	• Of countries • Of states
	2. scale	• In miles • In kilometers
	3. _____	
	4. _____	
	5. _____	
	6. _____	
	7. _____	
	8. _____	
	9. _____	
	10. _____	
	11. _____	
	12. _____	
	13. _____	

Mapping the State

by Chris Gustafson
NCSS 3, People, Places, Environments

Narrator 1: The class was spread out all over the library. A few students were using overhead projectors to trace maps of the state on big pieces of paper. Some others were doing research on the computers.

Narrator 2: Most of them were using pencils and rulers to add mountains, rivers, and cities to the maps they'd already traced.

Thuy: I do NOT get why we have to do this. This is the most stupid assignment I have ever done! I have never in my life gone to the eastern part of the state, so why do I have to learn about it?

Clarice: Because everyone has to learn state geography. That's so you won't sound stupid when you meet a cute guy from Sunnyside and you don't know where it is.

Thuy: I never meet any cute guys.

John: You know me. You don't need to meet any more.

Thuy: I don't think so!

Narrator 1: Thuy grabbed John's ruler and handed it to Clarice.

Narrator 2: Clarice hid the ruler under the table.

John: Hey! Now I can't make everything to scale.

Thuy: Oh, well!

Clarice: Thuy, what's your map theme?

Thuy: Huh?

Clarice: You know, you have to write a paragraph on something that's found in all regions of the state.

John: I'm doing airports. They're kind of boring, but I knew they'd be in all the regions.

Clarice: I was going to do prisons, but paintball parks are more fun. It's amazing; they're all over!

Thuy: I really don't get the point of this assignment. When my family goes on vacation, it's always to the same place, to see my grandma three hours south of here. It's boring.

Narrator 1: The teacher walked by, and Thuy concentrated on shading in the only river she'd drawn on her map.

Narrator 2: Then she kept talking, but a bit more quietly.

Thuy: It's not like I'll ever get to drive to any of these places myself when I get my license. Four kids in our family and one car! It's not going to happen.

John: So what's your theme, Thuy?

Thuy: How about volcanoes?

Clarice: Uh, is there one in each region? Try colleges, they're all over.

Narrator 1: Thuy found a free computer.

Narrator 2: Clarice was right. There were colleges all over the state, and they had cool Web pages. Thuy began to take notes.

Narrator 1: When Thuy came back to her table, she waved her paper at John and Clarice.

Thuy: Look at this! You won't believe it!

John: Won't believe what?

Narrator 2: John was using correction fluid to cover a big smear where he'd guessed wrong about the location of a mountain range.

John: I wouldn't have messed up if you hadn't taken my ruler!

Thuy: You were right, Clarice, colleges were easy. Look what I found at this one!

Narrator 1: Clarice looked at Thuy's paper.

Clarice: Something about a summer music camp. So what?

Thuy: Remember the solo I did at the last concert? The choir
director made a tape and gave me a copy. At this college
they have a summer music program for middle and high school students.
You have to send in a tape and they have scholarships!

John: What region is it in? Do you know any of the cities and rivers?

Clarice: Is it in that city with the cute guys?

Thuy: I don't know where it is! But it's on the list of cities we have to draw in.
Come on, you guys, help me find it!

Narrator 2: Thuy and Clarice and John stared at the map in their atlas.

Clarice: Here it is.

John: Where?

Clarice: About as far away from here as you can get and not be in the next state.

Thuy: All right!

Narrator 1: John looked at the map carefully.

John: It's not on a major river, so you'll have to forget about traveling there by canoe.

Clarice: It's got to be on a bus line.

Thuy: I'm going to download the music camp application. Put a dot on my map for
the city, Clarice. Thanks for the great idea.

Narrator 2: And Thuy handed John back his ruler.

Sitting Bull

by Chris Gustafson
NCSS 4, Individual Development and Identity

Sitting Bull was a Native American leader and warrior who lived in the late 1700s and early 1800s.

Introduction

Almost everything about white people shocked or puzzled the Lakota. The Lakota believed that dogs, not children, should be whipped, and thought that white children were abused. Whites and Lakotas had entirely different ideas about what property was for, and what it meant to own something. The clash of these two cultures resulted in tragedy.

Vocabulary Activity

Make an overhead of the *"Sitting Bull* Vocabulary" page, or give copies to groups of students or individuals. Tell students they are going to be doing a Reader's Theatre piece about the Native American leader, Sitting Bull. Ask students to cross out the words they don't think will be in the Reader's Theatre piece. Students will predict the meaning of the words they think will be included.

Vocabulary Words

coup—gaining prestige by touching but not injuring an opponent

cradleboard—a type of backpack for babies

Crows—a Native American tribe

detachment—group of soldiers split off from a larger group

Great Spirit—God

Lakota—a Native American tribe

news-walker—carries the news from village to village

Plains Indians—the Lakota were considered part of this group

Before Reading

Pass out the anticipation guide. Give students a few minutes to agree or disagree with each statement.

24

Perform *Sitting Bull*

Cast of Characters

> *Sitting Bull's Father, also named Sitting Bull—proud, loves his family*
> *Sitting Bull's Mother, Holy Door—firm, loving*
> *Sitting Bull—outrageously brave, thoughtful*
> *Red Cloud—a pragmatic chief*

After Reading

Give students a few minutes to revise their anticipation guides and write briefly why they changed their answers. Have students discuss in small groups how they responded to each statement, why they responded that way, and why they may have changed their answers. Then have them complete the character profile of Sitting Bull.

Additional Details

As Sitting Bull became a man in the late 1800s, there were more and more divisions among the Plains tribes. Should they make a deal with the whites and settle on reservations? Should they continue to fight for their old way of life? Sitting Bull found himself right in the middle of conflict between his people and the whites. He was not a man to back down.

Marrin, Albert, *Sitting Bull and His World*. Dutton Children's Books, 2000, 27 pp.

Sitting Bull Vocabulary

Cross out the eight words you don't think would be included in a Reader's Theatre piece about Sitting Bull. Write what you think the remaining eight words mean.

news-walker	cradleboard	Nootka	coup
potlatch	detachment	U.S. Navy	newspaper
California	warrior	Lakota	Crows
guns	Plains Indians	plenty	Great Spirit

Name _____ Period _____ Date _____

 Sitting Bull Anticipation Guide

	Agree	Disagree
1. The most important thing is to kill your enemy.		
2. Native American parents expected different things from their children than white settler parents did.		
3. Native American parents were kind to their children.		
4. Your name reflects who you are.		
5. Killing encourages revenge.		
6. At fourteen, you're a grown-up.		

- -

Name _____ Period _____ Date _____

 Sitting Bull Anticipation Guide

	Agree	Disagree
1. The most important thing is to kill your enemy.		
2. Native American parents expected different things from their children than white settler parents did.		
3. Native American parents were kind to their children.		
4. Your name reflects who you are.		
5. Killing encourages revenge.		
6. At fourteen, you're a grown-up.		

Sitting Bull

by Chris Gustafson
NCSS 4, Individual Development and Identity

Sitting Bull's Father, also named Sitting Bull: Each child is a blessing sent by the Great Spirit, and the birth of my son was an important event. I sent a news-walker among the other bands and tribes with the news, and many people came to his naming ceremony. I named him Jumping Badger, but soon he was nicknamed "Slow." Not because he was stupid, or clumsy, but because he was thoughtful. When other babies were given food, they ate it right away. Slow turned it over and studied it before putting it into his mouth.

Sitting Bull's Mother, Holy Door: Slow spent his first six months strapped in a cradleboard and he went everywhere with me. Once a day I bathed him, cleaned him, and changed the dried moss in the cradleboard. Like all Lakota children, he had a lot of freedom. Freedom to crawl around, to explore, even to get hurt. "One must learn from the bite of the fire to let it alone," Lakota parents say. But Lakota children are never allowed to cry. That might reveal the camp's location to our enemies. If cuddling or nursing doesn't stop the crying, I might pinch his nose closed and put my palm over his mouth.

Sitting Bull: I grew up learning about war. Plains Indians hunt to live, and they live to fight. Fighting and courage are the most important things, and honor is gained by risking your life. No woman would marry a man who had not proven himself in battle. I'll never forget my first battle against the Crows! I rode straight toward a warrior with his bow drawn. I whacked him across the arm, spoiling his aim, and the arrow flew off harmlessly. It was my first coup. My companions killed the warrior. My father was so proud of me that he gave away his horses. My father was so proud of me that he gave me his name, Sitting Bull. I was fourteen.

Red Cloud: I sent Sitting Bull to fight against the soldiers. There are white people all about me. I have but a small spot of land left, and the Great Spirit told me to keep it. A whole detachment was left dead on the hillside when Sitting Bull and the other warriors were through. That's what gave many of the white people the idea that they would have to kill us all.

Character Sheet — Sitting Bull

Likes:

_____

_____

_____

Dislikes:

_____

_____

_____

Hopes:

_____

_____

_____

Fears:

_____

_____

_____

Achievements:

_____

_____

_____

Other:

_____

_____

_____

Primary Sources

by Chris Gustafson
NCSS 5, Individuals, Groups, Institutions

Vocabulary Activity

Give each team of students a copy of the *"Primary Sources* Vocabulary" page. Ask students to cut apart the boxes, sort them into three or four groups, and give each group a title. Students explain to the rest of the class the reasons why they grouped their words as they did.

Vocabulary Words

booby-trapped—something harmful hidden in something that looks safe
Cambodia—a country in southeast Asia
eyewitness—person who gives a first-person account of an event
gardenia—a fragrant flower
graffiti—vandalizing by writing on the property of others
heritage—cultural background
Home Guard—local people who help the police
KKK—the Ku Klux Klan, a racist group
primary sources—historical accounts created at the time of an event, such as maps, posters, interviews, newspaper stories, diaries recounting events and reactions to events

Before Reading

Brainstorm with the class all the possible examples of primary sources.

30

Perform *Primary Sources*

Cast of Characters

Narrator 1
Narrator 2
Vincent—thoughtful
Anna—curious
Ms. Benetti—plans carefully

After Reading

Have students choose a primary source—a written, audio, or videotaped interview, a map, political cartoon, magazine article, newspaper article, government document, an advertisement, pamphlet, poster, legal decision, journal entry, personal letter, speech, financial record, photo, painting, or sculpture. Have students choose a less common type of primary source to describe a current or historical event. Work with students to create a grading standard to evaluate the product.

Primary Sources Vocabulary

KKK	gardenia	primary sources
heritage	booby-trapped	Cambodia
graffiti	Home Guard	eyewitness

Primary Sources

by Chris Gustafson
NCSS 5, Individuals, Groups, Institutions

Narrator 1: Vincent's class was meeting for a lesson in the library. He was saving a seat for Anna.

Vincent: What took you so long?

Anna: Briana booby-trapped my locker. When I opened it, almost a whole bottle of hand lotion spilled out. The counselor was down the hall and got all freaked out. She thought it was white paint on my locker, and that I was some sort of KKK target.

Vincent: Briana's not into that stuff! Plus, her parents are from Cambodia!

Anna: Everyone's jumpy after that racist graffiti last week. I convinced her that White Gardenia hand lotion wouldn't work for graffiti. It made my locker smell pretty good. Are we on for Saturday?

Vincent: Umm, I've got a little problem with my mom.

Ms. Benetti: I need your attention, class. Tell me what you know about primary sources. Vincent?

Vincent: Isn't that when you ask a little kid something?

Narrator 2: Anna was sitting next to Vincent. She started to giggle.

Ms. Benetti: Well, it could be. Only if the little kid was an eyewitness to something important.

Anna: My little brother thinks everything that happens to him is important. News flash! Devon blows his nose!

Ms. Benetti: Today we're going to learn about an event in our city from primary sources—what the people who were actually there wrote down. There are four stations around the library with an activity at each station. Read the directions carefully. You have one hour.

Narrator 1: Everyone else crowded around the first two stations, so Vincent headed for the third one. Anna plopped down in the chair next to him.

Vincent: So what do we do here?

Narrator 2: Anna read the directions out loud.

Anna: Look at the cartoon. Describe what is happening on the note-taking sheet. What is the point of view of the person who drew it? Use details from the drawing to support your answer.

Narrator 1: Vincent picked up the cartoon. It showed a group of white men in old-fashioned hats. Some had clubs and others had guns in their hands.

Narrator 2: They were standing around a group of Asian men. The Asian men were crouched down next to trunks and boxes. One of them was holding up his hands.

Vincent: See this guy? He looks like he's giving up.

Narrator 1: Anna read the caption under the cartoon.

Anna: "Home Guard Protects Chinese from a Mob, 1886."

Vincent: What's the Home Guard? Why is there a mob?

Anna: It doesn't say. Just write down what's happening.

Narrator 2: Anna took notes. Vincent stared at the picture.

Vincent: It's so strange. All the white men are kind of penciled in. They look solid. The Chinese are just outlines

Anna: Everyone looks angry and scared.

Narrator 1: Anna wrote some more.

Ms. Benetti: Time to move to another station.

Anna: Let's go, Vincent.

Narrator 2: Vincent slowly put the cartoon down. Anna pulled on his arm.

Anna: Over here!

Narrator 1: The next station had a copy of an interview.

Narrator 2: Vincent began to skim it.

Vincent: The Chinese were accepting lower wages than white men, so there was a big riot. Everyone had been picking on the Chinese workers and they were scared.

Narrator 1: Anna looked over Vincent's shoulder.

Anna: The mob was shouting, "The Chinese must go!"

Vincent: It says all three hundred and fifty Chinese in Seattle were herded to the dock at the end of Main Street where a boat was waiting.

Anna: By that time they were so scared one of them told a reporter that he wanted to leave.

Vincent: But the captain of the boat wanted seven dollars each. Only nine of the Chinese had enough money to pay the fare.

Anna: Not everyone could get on the boat that night, so the Home Guard tried to take some men back to their homes until the next boat came.

Vincent: Then someone in the mob grabbed a gun from one of the Home Guard and started shooting.

Narrator 2: Vincent and Anna studied the news article.

Anna: Did that happen to your family? When did they come to the United States?

Vincent: When my grandma and grandpa were in their twenties. It was way after this happened. I never knew about this!

Ms. Benetti: Okay everyone, finish up.

Anna: So, what about Saturday?

Vincent: My mom's been bugging me to come with her to the Asian Heritage Museum—she volunteers there. I didn't want to go, but now . . .

Anna: Could I come with you?

Narrator 1: Vincent picked up his binder.

Narrator 2: He walked toward the door with Anna.

Vincent: I think that would be great.

Anna: Call me.

Censoring the Newspaper

by Chris Gustafson
NCSS 6, Power, Authority, Governance

Vocabulary Activity

List the vocabulary words and phrases on the board, divide students into groups of four, and introduce vocabulary skits. Adjust the number of words and phrases to match your class, copy as many vocabulary pages as you need, and hand each group the directions for the skits with their vocabulary word or phrase written in the blank spot. They will act out a short scene that shows the meaning of their vocabulary word or phrase, during which the word or phrase itself may not be used. Each member of the group must act and speak during the skit. At the conclusion of each skit, the class will guess which word or phrase was being depicted. It may be helpful to set a few group rules for classroom drama. For example, there should be no physical contact between group members; do not depict scenes that violate school codes for violent or inappropriate behavior; those people you see on the screen are *acting*, that's not real blood, so what you show doesn't really have to be happening.

Vocabulary Words

Bill of Rights—the first ten amendments to the Constitution
censor—to suppress what is deemed objectionable
debate—to argue both sides of an issue
paralegal—trained legal assistant
podium—a place where a speaker can put notes, sometimes big enough to stand in
pumps—women's shoes that have medium or high heels and no fastenings
retrieve—get back
skim—go over quickly

Before Reading

As a class or in groups, create a mind map of everything the students know about censorship.

Perform *Censoring the Newspaper*

Cast of Characters

Narrator 1
Narrator 2
Ms. Castillo
McKenna—mocking
Roneel—all bluster
Peter—defensive
Jen—goes along with McKenna

After Reading

Have students complete the "Problems and Solutions" page. The first part of the page includes events from the Reader's Theatre script. The last part asks students to predict other problems the characters might encounter.

Fuller, Sarah, *Hazelwood v. Kulhmeier, Censorship in School Newspapers.*
    Enslow Publishers, Inc., 1998, 118 pp.

Name _____ Period _____ Date _____

 ## Censoring the Newspaper Vocabulary

With your group, think of a short scene that would *show* (not tell) the meaning of the vocabulary word or phrase you've been assigned. Everyone in the group must have an acting and a speaking part. Do not touch other cast members, say aloud the word or phrase you are acting out, or violate any school rules in your skit. Use a dictionary if no one in your group knows the meaning of the word or phrase you've been assigned.

Your word or phrase is:

_____

- -

Name _____ Period _____ Date _____

 ## Censoring the Newspaper Vocabulary

With your group, think of a short scene that would *show* (not tell) the meaning of the vocabulary word or phrase you've been assigned. Everyone in the group must have an acting and a speaking part. Do not touch other cast members, say aloud the word or phrase you are acting out, or violate any school rules in your skit. Use a dictionary if no one in your group knows the meaning of the word or phrase you've been assigned.

Your word or phrase is:

_____

- -

Name _____ Period _____ Date _____

 ## Censoring the Newspaper Vocabulary

With your group, think of a short scene that would *show* (not tell) the meaning of the vocabulary word or phrase you've been assigned. Everyone in the group must have an acting and a speaking part. Do not touch other cast members, say aloud the word or phrase you are acting out, or violate any school rules in your skit. Use a dictionary if no one in your group knows the meaning of the word or phrase you've been assigned.

Your word or phrase is:

_____

Censoring the Newspaper

by Chris Gustafson
NCSS 6, Power, Authority, Governance

Narrator 1: Ms. Castillo loved to teach the Bill of Rights.

Narrator 2: She organized her class into teams and sent them off to the library to research both sides of famous court cases. The teams were getting ready for a class debate.

McKenna: Roneel, you and Peter have no chance against Jen and me. Your side is so lame!

Jen: Yeah, no one in the class is going to vote that it's okay to censor a school newspaper.

Roneel: We didn't pick this side, but that's going to make it even better when the class listens to our arguments and decides that we're right.

Peter: Yeah, and my mom's a paralegal, and she's going to help us.

McKenna: You're not going to win, because censorship is wrong. Come on Jen, let's get to work.

Narrator 1: McKenna and Jen settled down next to each other and started to read.

Narrator 2: Jen had found a book on their court case. It was called *Hazelwood v. Kulhmeier.*

Jen: Look at this! This is so bogus! The principal read over the paper right before it was going to be printed and decided to pull two pages of stories about teen pregnancy.

McKenna: Here's the stories he censored. There's a factual one, some interviews, and a graph about teen pregnancy.

Jen: The principal never told the students what he didn't like; and he didn't give them a chance to fix the articles.

McKenna: Like they would have! The articles were fine the way they were!

Narrator 2: Roneel and Peter had pulled some information on the case from the internet.

Roneel: Wow, look! This is pretty cool. The Supreme Court ruled in favor of our side.

Peter: I can't believe they actually said it was okay to censor a student newspaper. That makes me feel kind of crummy. Isn't it illegal to censor regular newspapers?

Roneel: I guess the first amendment is different when it's a school newspaper. Because it's a class, the teachers and administrators can decide not to print stuff even if the students think it's okay.

Peter: Roneel, I think I agree with McKenna. This censorship thing is really wrong.

Roneel: Peter, get over it! This is going to be fun. The girls are going to get all mad at us; but we'll have the best arguments, so we'll win.

Peter: Well, my mom did say to be sure we have persuasive reasons on our side. There are some good ones in this article.

Narrator 1: Peter pulled out his purple highlighter and began to read the article.

Narrator 2: McKenna and Jen wrote down the arguments they found for their side.

Jen: Oh, crud, look at this!

McKenna: What?

Jen: Read this last paragraph. Our side lost!

McKenna: They lost? You're kidding. That is totally not possible! The Supreme Court decided that censorship was okay?

Narrator 1: Jen pointed at a list in the book.

Jen: These are the arguments the court agreed with. Our side lost.

McKenna: This is kind of an old case. What happened later?

Narrator 2: Jen skimmed the next page.

Jen: It says there have been many court cases based on censorship of student newspapers since then, but the Supreme Court has never reversed its ruling.

McKenna: We are toast. What are we going to do?

Narrator 1: Jen turned the last page of the book and slammed it down on the table.

Jen: We're going to take every one of those arguments and explain why they're wrong. I know we can persuade the class! We just have to work hard and know our stuff.

Narrator 2: On the day of the debate, Jen and McKenna and Peter and Roneel faced off in front of the class.

Narrator 1: Each team had a podium to hold their notes. There would be time for an opening statement, the oral arguments, and concluding statements.

Narrator 2: Peter pulled at the knot of his tie. He didn't want to sound like he was choking. He faced the class and made eye contact with everyone, just like his mom had told him.

Peter: Ladies and gentlemen of the jury, by the time this debate is over, I'm sure you'll agree the Supreme Court made a wise choice when they ruled for the school administration in the case of *Hazelwood v. Kulhmeier.*

Narrator 1: McKenna moved her feet inside her mother's pumps. They were a little bit big, but her running shoes would have looked dumb with her mother's suit. She leaned over just a little to whisper to Jen.

McKenna: I don't think so!

Narrator 2: The girls stood up straight, listened to Peter, and waited for their turn.

Censoring the Newspaper Problems and Solutions

In the Reader's Theatre, find the problems to match the solutions that are listed. Then imagine what might happen to the characters after the play ends. Write two problems they might face there, and a possible solution for each of those problems.

1. **Problem:** _____

   Solution: The principal in the court case censored the student newspaper.

2. **Problem:** _____

   Solution: The Supreme Court ruled in favor of the principal.

3. **Problem:** _____

   Solution: Peter and Roneel worked hard to present evidence for their side.

4. **Problem:** _____

   Solution: McKenna and Jen tried to refute every argument in the Supreme Court decision.

Imagine what might happen during the time the two teams present their arguments.

5. **Problem:** _____

   Solution: _____

6. **Problem:** _____

   Solution: _____

Snapshots from the Great Depression

by Chris Gustafson
NCSS 7, Production, Distribution, Consumption

Vocabulary Activity

Divide the class into teams or groups. Assign a vocabulary word to each team or group, and give them a short time to agree on a definition to briefly present to the class.

Vocabulary Words

drought—a long time without rain

Great Depression—a time of intense economic hardship worldwide, primarily during the late 1920s through the early 1930s

Hooverville—communities of thrown-together shacks that sheltered the very poor during the Great Depression

lottery—a drawing to win something against long odds

Philippines—a country made up of a group of islands off the coast of southeast Asia

Prozac—a medicine taken for depression

stock market crash—when stocks plummet in value

Before Reading

Individually, in groups, or as a class, have students complete the first two sections of the KWL chart about the Great Depression. Since this age group is likely to answer the question, "What do you want to know?" with a resounding "Nothing," try using the phrase "What do you wonder?" for the middle part of the chart.

Perform *Snapshots from the Great Depression*

Cast of Characters

> *Narrator 1*
> *Narrator 2*
> *Eliot—good sense of humor*
> *Louisa—kindhearted*
> *Jack—likes glitz*
> *Rebecca—serious, shy*

After Reading

Fill in the final section of the KWL chart. On the back, have students draw a picture suggested by one of the scenes described in the Reader's Theatre piece. Work with students to create a grading standard that describes the best possible picture.

Name _____ Period _____ Date _____

KWL/The Great Depression

What I Know About the Great Depression	What I Wonder About the Great Depression	What I Learned About the Great Depression

Snapshots from the Great Depression

by Chris Gustafson

NCSS 7, Production, Distribution, Consumption

Narrator 1: In the past several weeks, Mr. Orlov's class had read general information about the Great Depression in their textbook. They had watched several films in class, and they had done some reading and research on their own.

Narrator 2: They had written personal responses to what they'd learned. Eliot, Louisa, Jack, and Rebecca were scheduled to share.

Eliot: When we started learning about the Great Depression, I knew absolutely nothing. Remember when we were supposed to write down what we already knew? My pencil didn't even get near the paper! When we were supposed to write down what we wondered, I did have one question. Didn't they have any counselors? What about Prozac? It sounded like a serious mental health issue! I decided to focus on life in the city, and I read this book called *Nothing to Fear*. That's what made the Depression seem real to me. My dad was out of work for a couple of months last year, but it wasn't really any big deal. Back then, men looked and looked for work, and couldn't find any for years. Lots of them left their families to try to find work somewhere else and send money back. Their wives did just about any kind of job to get by, like sewing or doing laundry. Kids had to work, shining shoes or carrying packages for pay, anything.

Louisa: When I was little, I used to go and visit my uncle's wheat farm every summer. It was always hot and the wind had this special, wheaty kind of smell. I wanted to find out more about what happened to the farmers during the depression. Things got bad on the farms even before the stock market crash—that was a big surprise. Farmers gambled that demand for food would keep increasing after World War I was over, but then they grew too much and that drove down prices. It's so confusing that they worked so hard and ended up making less money. Then there was a drought, and farmers couldn't even grow enough to feed themselves. Parents had to watch their kids go hungry and get skinnier and skinnier. In one town, the farmers got desperate. They all went to the town store and threatened to break in and steal food. The store owner just gave it to them. I don't know how the owner paid for the food. Why wouldn't anyone help the farmers?

Jack: I liked the movie we saw in class about all the rich people in the twenties. They were really kind of crazy. They built those huge houses and lived like royalty. And the really weird thing is that they weren't exactly doing work to get all that money. I mean, at the end of the day they couldn't say they'd taught somebody something, or designed a building, or cleaned an apartment, or cooked a burger. In a way, they were just gamblers in the stock market, and they totally encouraged everyone else to gamble in the stock market too. Everyone actually seemed to believe you could get something for nothing. The whole culture, movie stars and singers, and even astrologers had this whole focus on the stock market and getting rich quick; but it seems like no one really knew what they were doing. As far as I could tell, when the market crashed, everyone was totally surprised. I'm not sure that much has changed when I see my dad buy a lottery ticket!

Rebecca: I didn't say anything at first, because I was really embarrassed. But when I saw those old, black and white photos of Hoovervilles, I knew I'd actually been there. Remember the places where homeless people built shacks out of anything during the Depression and named them after President Hoover? Last summer, I went to the Philippines for the first time to visit my uncle, aunt, and cousins. On the way to their house our bus passed by a place that looked just like the Hooverville pictures. Just exactly, except it was in color, and I could see women hanging up their laundry with little kids running around. It was crowded, sort of dirty, and I felt ashamed that the country my family came from had such poor people. But when I studied about the Depression, I figured out that no matter how hard people try, sometimes the economy fails, and lots of people suffer. It's not really their fault.

Benjamin Franklin

by Chris Gustafson
NCSS 8, Science, Technology, Society

Benjamin Franklin was a diplomat, politician, inventor, and author during the late 1700s in the United States.

Vocabulary Activity

Have students individually fill out the "What I Know About Benjamin Franklin Vocabulary" page. Then have them work in groups to fill in the meanings of any words of which they aren't sure.

Vocabulary Words

bifocals—glasses with an insert for viewing close objects and text
epidemic—a large outbreak of disease in a particular area
friction—rubbing one object against another
inoculation—a shot that delivers a vaccine against a disease
jutted—stuck out
smallpox—a deadly disease

Before Reading

Using the taxonomy page, as a class, individually, or in groups, have students fill in as many words starting with each letter as they can about the life and times of Benjamin Franklin.

Benjamin Franklin *(continued)*

Perform *Benjamin Franklin*

Cast of Characters

> *James Franklin—Benjamin's brother, strict, jealous*
> *Deborah Franklin—Benjamin's wife, loving, constant, steady*
> *Benjamin Franklin—curious and energetic*
> *Sally Franklin—Benjamin's daughter, admiring, loving*

After Reading

Have students add any new words they can to the taxonomy page. Teach students the three-level questioning strategy—how to look for information that is right there, for which they have to think and search, and for more open-ended questions when they are on their own. Students will apply the strategy using the "Three-level Questions" page.

Adler, David, *B. Franklin*, Printer. Holiday House, 2001, 103 pp.

Fish, Bruce and Becky, *Benjamin Franklin, American Statesman, Scientist, and Writer*,
   Chelsea House, 2000, 70 pp.

Name _____ Period _____ Date _____

What I Know About Benjamin Franklin Vocabulary

Vocabulary Word	I have never heard of this word.	I've heard of this word but I'm not sure what it means.	I know this word. It means . . .
smallpox			
inoculation			
epidemic			
jutted			
friction			
bifocals			

Benjamin Franklin Taxonomy

A _____
_____

B _____
_____

C _____
_____

D _____
_____

E _____
_____

F _____
_____

G _____
_____

H _____
_____

I _____
_____

J _____
_____

K _____
_____

L _____
_____

M _____
_____

N _____
_____

O _____
_____

P _____
_____

Q _____

R _____
_____

S _____
_____

T _____
_____

U _____
_____

V _____
_____

W _____
_____

X _____

Y _____

Z _____

Benjamin Franklin

by Chris Gustafson
NCSS 8, Science, Technology, Society

James Franklin, Benjamin's Brother: My father wanted my brother to work in his soap and candle shop. But Benjamin never liked the work. He wanted to run away and go to sea, which really worried our father. So he asked me to take Benjamin on as an apprentice in my print shop. I had just gotten my own type and printing press. He worked hard, and I taught him everything he needed to know. But he was never content just to be a printer. I found out that he had been writing letters to the newspaper I published and signing a different name. He was only sixteen years old! When I found out, I felt like he made a fool of me. We fought more and more. When he quit, I told all the other printers in Boston not to hire him.

Deborah Franklin, Benjamin's Wife: I didn't know what to think about smallpox inoculations. When our son, Francis, was born, we wondered if we should have him inoculated. It is such a strange idea! To deliberately give our precious Francis a bit of smallpox to keep him from getting a more serious case. What if it didn't work? It would be like killing our own son; so we didn't do it. But when Francis was four, there was a smallpox epidemic in Philadelphia, and he died. Everyone knew my husband was interested in the idea of inoculations. A rumor went around that we had had Francis inoculated and it didn't work. It wasn't true. My husband and I were heartbroken. I wish we HAD inoculated Francis.

Benjamin Franklin: Nothing is as amazing as the study of electricity! I put together a lab in my house to experiment with this powerful, invisible force. If you get a jar half full of water and put one end of the wire in the water, you create friction at the other end of the wire, and you can store electricity. I began to experiment with using electricity to kill chickens. Killing a turkey took a lot more current! That's how I got interested in finding out more about lightning. You all know what happened with the kite and the key!

Sally Franklin, Benjamin's Daughter: I never met a man as curious as my father. He wondered if a metal stove that jutted out a bit from the fireplace would keep a room warmer, so he built one. It did! He invented a kind of eye glasses with two different types of lenses; one was for close up work and one for looking far away. He liked to make those magic math squares where all the numbers always add up to the same total; but they didn't always come out quite right. He never stopped asking himself, "What if?" And he never stopped trying to make things better.

Name _____ Period _____ Date _____

 # Three-Level Questions About *Benjamin Franklin*

Answer each question in complete sentences on a separate piece of paper.

1. Where did Benjamin's father want him to work? *(right there)*

2. What did Benjamin do to annoy his brother? *(think and search)*

3. Why do you think his parents decided not to inoculate Francis? *(on your own)*

4. How do inoculations work? *(think and search)*

5. How did Franklin experiment with electricity? *(right there)*

6. What are some of Franklin's inventions? *(think and search)*

7. If Franklin were alive today, what problems do you think he would be trying to solve? Why would he be trying to solve them? *(on your own)*

- -

Name _____ Period _____ Date _____

 # Three-Level Questions About *Benjamin Franklin*

Answer each question in complete sentences on a separate piece of paper.

1. Where did Benjamin's father want him to work? *(right there)*

2. What did Benjamin do to annoy his brother? *(think and search)*

3. Why do you think his parents decided not to inoculate Francis? *(on your own)*

4. How do inoculations work? *(think and search)*

5. How did Franklin experiment with electricity? *(right there)*

6. What are some of Franklin's inventions? *(think and search)*

7. If Franklin were alive today, what problems do you think he would be trying to solve? Why would he be trying to solve them? *(on your own)*

Francs for Burkina Faso

by Chris Gustafson
NCSS 9, Global Connections

Vocabulary Activity

The vocabulary page asks students to read new vocabulary words and then analyze three words or phrases. Two of the words or phrases relate to the meaning of the vocabulary word; one does not. Students will cross out the word or phrase that does not relate, then write a brief explanation of why the remaining words go together.

Vocabulary Words

Burkina Faso—a land-locked country in west Africa

colony—a country whose economy and government are controlled by another country

Culturegrams—four-page brochures with information about individual countries (not on the vocabulary sheet but may need explaining)

Euro—European currency usable in many European countries

foreign aid—money or other assistance given by one country to another

franc—pre-Euro French currency, still used in some former French colonies

France—a country in western Europe

life expectancy—how many years people are expected to live

Before Reading

Copy and cut up the squares on the "Types of Foreign Aid" page. Have each student draw a square and share aloud one specific way a more developed country could help a less developed country in the area described on the square.

Perform *Francs for Burkina Faso*

Cast of Characters

> *Narrator 1*
> *Narrator 2*
> *Kevin—open to new ideas, creative*
> *Teenah—smug, not too thoughtful*
> *Mr. Johanson—keeps things moving*

After Reading

Tell your students that they have each been given the job of allocating foreign aid to a particular country and they have ten million dollars to give to their country. Assign a country to each student or team of students, and ask them to skim the CIA Factbook (http://www.cia.gov/cia/publications/factbook/) for information on their country. Using that information, they are to decide how their ten million dollars could help their country the most. The money must be spent on at least two but no more than four types of aid. Students will write a brief paper allocating the money and explaining their choices. Work with students to create a grading standard to describe the best possible persuasive paper.

Culturegrams, *Burkina Faso*. Millennial Star Network and Brigham Young University, 2001.

Francs for Burkina Faso Vocabulary

Cross out the word or phrase that does not relate to the vocabulary word. Explain how the two remaining words or phrases relate to each other.

1. **foreign aid**   money   advisors   birth rate

_____

2. **colony**   United States Virginia   Oregon

_____

3. **Euro**   franc   dollar   travel guide

_____

4. **France**   California   Iceland   Burkina Faso

_____

5. **life expectancy** disease   teenagers   nutrition

_____

Name _____ Period _____ Date _____

Types of Foreign Aid

Disease Prevention	Agriculture	Medicine	Food Distribution	Small Business
Disease Prevention	Agriculture	Medicine	Food Distribution	Small Business
Disease Prevention	Agriculture	Medicine	Food Distribution	Small Business
Disease Prevention	Agriculture	Medicine	Food Distribution	Small Business
Disease Prevention	Agriculture	Medicine	Food Distribution	Small Business
Disease Prevention	Agriculture	Medicine	Food Distribution	Small Business

Francs for Burkina Faso

by Chris Gustafson
NCSS 9, Global Connections

Narrator 1: Kevin and Treenah sat across from each other at a table in the library.

Narrator 2: The table was covered with encyclopedia volumes, notecards, and books.

Kevin: What country are you doing for your report?

Treenah: France. My older sister went to France with the French Club last year. I want to go, too. She had an amazing time! How about you?

Kevin: Burkina Faso.

Treenah: Burkina Faso? Where's that? Why did you pick it?

Kevin: It's in Africa. I wanted to learn about a country there, and it's got kind of a crazy name. It sounded cool.

Treenah: Is it turning out to be cool?

Kevin: I haven't done much research yet. It's really hot and landlocked. But it's got some pretty big rivers.

Mr. Johanson: Everyone needs to check the front of the project sheet. Once you've gotten some basic information about your country, you have a decision to make. Imagine that your country has received a foreign aid grant from the United States. Part of your project is your foreign aid application. You'll need to choose the top five places where you'd spend the foreign aid and explain your choices.

Treenah: The French university system sounds great. It says in this Culturegram that it's practically free. Maybe I could go there for college.

Narrator 1: Kevin picked up his Culturegram and read the section on education.

Kevin: Well, if you know French, you could go to school in Burkina Faso. School is in French, which is really stupid, because that's not what most people speak.

Treenah: How come?

Kevin: I don't know.

Narrator 2: Treenah opened an encyclopedia, and Kevin scanned the history part of the Culturegram.

Kevin: Hey, here's why! Burkina Faso was a colony of France. The French decided on their borders and took over the economy and schools and the government. I guess they wanted everything to be in French.

Treenah: Well, it is a beautiful language.

Kevin: So's Spanish, but if you told me tomorrow I'd have to do all my schoolwork in Spanish, I'd fail everything. Lots of kids in Burkina Faso do crummy in school and drop out because they don't know how to speak French.

Treenah: Sounds like that's where you should use your foreign aid, then.

Mr. Johanson: If you've been using the computer for research, switch to print materials. If you haven't had a turn on the computer, take it now.

Narrator 1: Kevin found a free computer and began a search.

Narrator 2: Soon his notetaking organizer filled up with information.

Narrator 1: Treenah sat at a computer across from Kevin.

Narrator 2: Kevin peered at Treenah around the monitor and hissed at her.

Kevin: Life expectancy in Burkina Faso is about 45 years. More than one out of ten babies die when they're really little. Being ruled by the French really . . .

Treenah: Don't blame it on me! What am I supposed to do about it?

Narrator 1: Treenah disappeared behind her monitor.

Narrator 2: Kevin passed Treenah a note. She unfolded it and read it.

Treenah: What do you mean, "Give me a franc."

Kevin: Just what I said. When your sister came back from France, did she bring any French money? She must have. Bring me a franc.

Treenah: You're crazy. What do you want a franc for?

Kevin: Just ask her, okay?

Narrator 1: Treenah shrugged.

Treenah: Okay, I'll ask.

Mr. Jacobson: Before you leave, I want everyone to turn to the presentation requirements on the assignment sheet. See where it says "Country in a Bag"? You'll bring a paper bag with ten small items that represent what you've learned about your country. As your oral presentation, you'll pull each of the items out of the bag and explain to the class how it relates to what you learned about your country.

Narrator 2: The day of Kevin's presentation, his stomach felt jumpy, and he wished he hadn't eaten strawberry yogurt for lunch.

Narrator 1: Treenah had given her presentation the day before. She had a lot of things in her bag that her sister had brought back from France. When she was finished, she handed Kevin a franc.

Treenah: You can keep it. They've already started using the Euro in France.

Narrator 2: Now Kevin pulled the franc from his bag, took a deep breath, and looked out over the class.

Narrator 1: He held up the franc so that everyone could see it.

Kevin: You already know what this is. Treenah showed you what French money used to look like yesterday. My country, Burkina Faso, was a colony of France, and when the French left, they left some major problems behind. In Burkina Faso, their money is still called the franc.

Narrator 2: Kevin looked at Mr. Jacobson.

Kevin: Mr. Jacobson, I'm going to use the rest of the objects in my bag to prove that because of the way France treated Burkina Faso, Burkina Faso should get the foreign aid grant that was set aside for France.

Treenah: No fair! I had plans for that money!

Mr. Jacobson: Go ahead, Kevin. Make your case.

Narrator 1: Kevin smiled.

Narrator 2: He pulled the second item out of his bag.

Trombone-Assisted Service Learning

by Chris Gustafson
NCSS 10, Civic Ideals and Practices

Vocabulary Activity

On the vocabulary page, students will draw a cartoon illustrating the meaning of each of the vocabulary words.

Vocabulary Words

fiction—a written work created by the imagination of the writer

foster children—kids who are living with other families because their own families can't take care of them

notetaking organizer—a worksheet for taking notes organized by source or topic

service learning—meeting learning goals while performing a service that benefits others

Before Reading

Is there a service learning requirement in your school district? If there isn't, should there be? Have students formally or informally debate these questions.

Perform *Trombone-Assisted Service Learning*

Cast of Characters

Narrator 1

Narrator 2

Binh—initially reluctant

Lily—interested, involved

Mr. Nguyen—compassionate

After Reading

Students use the pro and con graphic organizer to set out reasons for and against a service learning requirement. Assign a five-paragraph persuasive essay supporting one of the two positions.

61

Trombone-Assisted Service Learning Vocabulary

Draw a cartoon in each of the boxes below to illustrate the vocabulary words.

service learning	foster children
notetaking organizer	**fiction**

Trombone-Assisted Service Learning

by Chris Gustafson
NCSS 10, Civil Ideals and Practices

Narrator 1: Binh and Lily were wandering through the fiction section of the library.

Narrator 2: Binh was holding a list of books.

Binh: I don't get it! I thought this was supposed to be the start of our service learning project. Why are we looking at novels?

Lily: Did you come in late? Mr. Nguyen explained it. We're supposed to read a book that has some sort of current problem in it—child abuse, parents who use drugs, depression, or something. Then there's a group part. I kind of missed that.

Binh: Oh, yeah, the groups. You get in a group with someone who read a book with the same kind of problem, like divorce or poverty, and then you do research about it. That's the group project.

Lily: Let me see your list. Have you read any of these books?

Binh: I don't think so. I guess I'll just find one that looks good and try it.

Mr. Nguyen: Okay everyone, ten more minutes to find a book. You'll need to finish reading it by the end of the month.

Narrator 1: Three weeks later, Binh and Lily were back in the library with their class.

Narrator 2: There was a big paper in front of the library with a list of current problems. Binh and Lily each wrote their name down under "Foster Children."

Lily: Was your book good?

Binh: Yeah, I was kind of surprised. It was about a boy who is living as a foster child in a family that adopted his little brother. The little brother doesn't even remember their parents, but the big brother wants to find the other three kids in the family and get everyone back together.

Lily: Does he?

Binh: Not really. He finds the other kids, but then he has to face up to how his parents died. He's been telling everyone they were in a car accident, but they really got AIDS from using drugs. I almost put my name down for the AIDS group.

Lily: Mine was just about foster care. This kid kept doing awful things to his foster family to see if they really wanted to keep him.

Mr. Nguyen: Listen up, people. You should be sitting with the others who signed under the same current problem topic. In a minute I'm going to hand out your service learning project paper and the grading standard. Briefly, each group will create a poster with summaries of the fiction books you read and information about your current problem. There's a list of information you'll need to include on your project paper.

Lily: Mr. Nguyen, why do we have to make a poster? Can't we just do an oral report?

Mr. Nguyen: The posters will go up in the halls because the information on them might be helpful to other students in our school. That's why you need to be sure to have a local phone number on the poster—a place where people can find out more or get help. The posters will go up in two weeks.

Narrator 1: Lily and Binh were the only people in the foster child group.

Narrator 2: They decided to divide up the work.

Lily: I'll look for the local stuff on the internet.

Binh: Okay. I'll look for any books here in the library.

Narrator 1: They gathered up their notetaking organizers and went to work.

Narrator 2: Two weeks later, Lily, Binh, and the rest of their class were taping their posters up in the hall across from the library.

Lily: Ours looks great! I like that photo you cut out of the newspaper of that foster care family.

Binh: The word-processed part is excellent. And putting the phone numbers on tear-off tabs was a good idea.

Lily: I tore off one to kind of get it started, so it would look like people are already interested.

Mr. Nguyen: Come over to the library everyone. It's time to plan the last part of our project.

Narrator 1: The class trickled in to the library.

Narrator 2: Binh was the last to get there. He had been putting a final tape roll on the back of the poster to be sure it would stay up.

Mr. Nguyen: Now it's time for the service learning piece of the project. You've read about your current problem, you've gathered information and made a poster. Next you'll plan a way your group can volunteer to help. Go ahead and meet to do some brainstorming.

Lily: Great! Now we're supposed to do something! It's not like we could take care of a foster child. Besides, that kid in the book I read was really mean to his family.

Binh: The kid in my book was nice enough, just really sad.

Lily: I can't even imagine what it would be like not to have a family to take care of me. Sometimes I fight with my mom, but I don't want to live somewhere else!

Binh: I don't think we have to fix everything. Just find one thing, maybe a little way to help.

Narrator 1: Lily and Binh began to write down all their ideas.

Narrator 2: Lily made Binh write down even the ones that sounded stupid.

Binh: Make parents go to classes so they'd be good parents.

Lily: Get rid of drugs.

Binh: Not let any parents die.

Lily: This is no use!

Mr. Nguyen: How's it going, you two?

Lily: Crummy. None of our ideas will work.

Narrator 1: Mr. Nguyen looked over their list.

Mr. Nguyen: Maybe you could start a little smaller. What do you think are some things you take for granted that might be hard for foster kids?

Narrator 2: Lily and Binh looked over their list again.

Lily: I would really miss my soccer team if I was in a foster family. And my trombone. There might not be enough money for stuff like that.

Binh: I could never give up my gymnastics lessons.

Lily: Let's look on the internet. Maybe there's some group already helping foster kids that we could help.

Narrator 1: Binh found ChildHelp, a local group that raises money to pay for the kinds of extras that foster families can't afford.

Narrator 2: For two weeks, Lily and Binh waited outside the lunchroom, collecting spare change.

Binh: Keep playing your trombone, Lily. Every time you do, we get more money in the cup.

Lily: Maybe they're just hoping I'll stop.

Binh: Naw. You sound okay.

Narrator 1: Binh rattled the change he'd collected in Lily's pencil box.

Binh: Fork over your change! Help kids in foster care!

Narrator 2: Lily smiled at Binh.

Narrator 1: Binh smiled back.

Pro and Con Service Learning Requirements

Pro Service Learning Requirements	Introduction	Details for:
	Reason One	Reason One
	Reason Two	Reason Two
	Reason Three	Reason Three
	Conclusion	
Con Service Learning Requirements	**Introduction**	**Details for:**
	Reason One	Reason One
	Reason Two	Reason Two
	Reason Three	Reason Three
	Conclusion	

National Standards for English and Language Arts

1 Students read a wide range of print and non-print texts to build an understanding of texts, of themselves, and of the cultures of the United States and the world; to acquire new information; to respond to the needs and demands of society and the workplace; and for personal fulfillment. Among these texts are fiction and nonfiction, classic and contemporary works.

2 Students read a wide range of literature from many periods in many genres to build an understanding of the many dimensions (e.g., philosophical, ethical, aesthetic) of human experience.

3 Students apply a wide range of strategies to comprehend, interpret, evaluate, and appreciate texts. They draw on their prior experience, their interactions with other readers and writers, their knowledge of word meanings and of other texts, their word identification strategies, and their understanding of textual features (e.g., sound-letter correspondence, sentence structure, context, graphics).

4 Students adjust their use of spoken, written, and visual language (e.g., conventions, style, vocabulary) to communicate effectively with a variety of audiences and for different purposes.

5 Students employ a wide range of strategies as they write and use different writing process elements appropriately to communicate with different audiences for a variety of purposes.

6 Students apply knowledge of language structure, language conventions (e.g., spelling and punctuation), media techniques, figurative language, and genre to create, critique, and discuss print and non-print texts.

7 Students conduct research on issues and interests by generating ideas and questions, and by posing problems. They gather, evaluate, and synthesize data from a variety of sources (e.g., print and non-print texts, artifacts, people) to communicate their discoveries in ways that suit their purpose and audience.

8 Students use a variety of technological and information resources (e.g., libraries, databases, computer networks, video) to gather and synthesize information and to create and communicate knowledge.

9 Students develop an understanding of and respect for diversity in language use, patterns, and dialects across cultures, ethnic groups, geographic regions, and social roles.

10 Students whose first language is not English make use of their first language to develop understanding of content across the curriculum.

11 Students participate as knowledgeable, reflective, creative, and critical members of a variety of literacy communities.

12 Students use spoken, written, and visual language to accomplish their own purposes (e.g., for learning, enjoyment, persuasion, and the exchange of information).

Standards for the English Language Arts, by the International Reading Association and the National Council of Teachers of English, Copyright 1996 by the International Reading Association and the National Council of Teachers of English. Reprinted with permission.

68

Theseus and the Minotaur

adapted by Chris Gustafson
NCTE Standard 1

Vocabulary Activity

Divide the class into 13 groups. Each group will need a dictionary, and three groups (those looking up Aegean Sea, Athens, and Crete) will need an atlas as well. Give each group five minutes to find the meaning of their word or phrase. Ask a spokesperson from each group to teach the rest of the class about their word or phrase in two or three complete sentences. Make an overhead of the *"Theseus and the Minotaur* Vocabulary" page and have a recorder write each definition next to the word or phrase, or copy the page so each student can write in the definitions.

Vocabulary Words

Aegean Sea—a body of water between Greece and Turkey

Athens—a city in Greece

Crete—an island off Greece

gleefully—gladly

grieve—to mourn

labyrinth—like a maze

maze—a twisty set of passages with many dead ends

Minotaur—half-bull, half-man, human flesh-eating

mourning—deep sorrow

occasional—every once in a while

provisions—food, supplies

roused—came to attention

tribute—a bribe or ransom

Before Reading

Pass out the anticipation guide. Give students a few minutes to agree or disagree with each statement.

69

Theseus and the Minotaur *(continued)*

Perform *Theseus and the Minotaur*

Cast of Characters

Narrator 1
Narrator 2
King Minos of Crete—cruel, wealthy, arrogant, manipulative
Prince Theseus of Athens—young, intrepid, vain, brave, immature
King of Athens—caught between a rock and a hard place
Princess Ariadne—clever, helpful, willing

After Reading

Give students a few minutes to revise their anticipation guides and write briefly why they changed their answers. Have students discuss in small groups how they responded to each statement, why they responded that way, and why they may have changed their answers.

Use the storytelling organizer to have students jot down the main events in the story. Have students practice telling the story until the details are firmly fixed in their minds. Each student can tell the story once to a partner for feedback on the storytelling feedback form. The final storytelling performance could be for a study buddy from a younger class.

D'Aulaire, Ingri and Edgar Parin, *Book of Greek Myths*. Bantam Doubleday Dell
    Publishing Group, 1963.

McCaughrean, Geraldine, *Greek Myths*. Macmillan Publishing Company, 1993, 96 pp.

Theseus and the Minotaur Vocabulary

Aegean Sea	gleefully	occasional
provisions	Minotaur	roused
tribute	Crete	grieve
mourning	labyrinth	maze
Athens		

Theseus and the Minotaur Anticipation Guide

	Agree	Disagree
1. All kings are equally powerful.		
2. Bold people are often foolish.		
3. It's a good idea to help someone, even if you know your parents wouldn't approve.		
4. Good looks are more important than helpfulness.		
5. It's okay to trick someone to get your own way.		
6. Not paying attention to details can have bad consequences.		

- -

Name _____ Period _____ Date _____

Theseus and the Minotaur Anticipation Guide

	Agree	Disagree
1. All kings are equally powerful.		
2. Bold people are often foolish.		
3. It's a good idea to help someone, even if you know your parents wouldn't approve.		
4. Good looks are more important than helpfulness.		
5. It's okay to trick someone to get your own way.		
6. Not paying attention to details can have bad consequences.		

Theseus and the Minotaur

adapted by Chris Gustafson
NCTE Standard 1

Narrator 1: King Minos of Crete was the most powerful king among many other kings in the ancient world. He was so powerful that neighboring kingdoms paid him tribute every year so that he would leave them alone.

Narrator 2: The neighboring kingdoms feared the maze King Minos had built. In the maze, King Minos kept a monster called the Minotaur. The hungry Minotaur preferred to eat the flesh of humans.

Narrator 1: Prince Theseus lived in a neighboring kingdom. When he became old enough, he asked his father, the King of Athens, why there was a time of sadness and mourning in their kingdom every spring.

King of Athens: It is the time when we must send tribute to King Minos of Crete.

Prince Theseus: Why must we send tribute to Crete?

King of Athens: King Minos is very powerful. He will attack us if we do not send the tribute.

Prince Theseus: Our people give tribute to you, father. They give fat bulls and a part of their harvest. But they do not grieve.

King of Athens: King Minos requires that we send him seven men and seven women to be fed to his fearful, flesh-eating monster, the Minotaur.

Prince Theseus: That's not right! Send me this year. I will kill the Minotaur and break the power of King Minos.

Narrator 1: The King of Athens did not want to send his son to Crete. But Prince Theseus insisted.

Narrator 2: Just before the ship set sail for Crete, the King said a final farewell to his son.

King of Athens: I will be watching for your return from the cliffs. If your trip is successful, raise a white sail for your trip home. If you fail, tell the sailors to keep using the old, black sail.

Prince Theseus: Don't worry father. I won't fail!

Narrator 1: King Minos gleefully welcomed the boat of tribute from Athens.

King Minos: Who'll go first to meet my Minotaur?

Prince Theseus: I, the Prince of Athens, will go first.

King Minos: You are bold but foolish.

Narrator 2: King Minos gave the order. Prince Theseus was hauled off toward the labyrinth.

Narrator 1: King Minos's daughter, Ariadne, had been listening. She hated the way her father fed young people to the Minotaur. She was unhappy on Crete. She felt even worse when she saw the brave and handsome Prince Theseus.

Narrator 2: As Prince Theseus was dragged by her, Ariadne thrust a magical ball of string into his hand. She whispered to him.

Princess Ariadne: Take this magical string! It may help you find your way out of the maze if you can kill the Minotaur. But if you succeed, you must marry me and take me away from here.

Narrator 1: Prince Theseus had no time to say anything but thank you.

Narrator 2: The guards dumped him at the opening of the maze and closed the gate. Theseus fastened the magical string at the entrance.

Narrator 1: He could hear the occasional hungry roars of the Minotaur as he felt his way down the dark passages, playing out the string.

Prince Theseus: The roars have stopped. But what's this? It's covered with coarse fur. Oh, no!

Narrator 2: The Minotaur roused himself and began to bite and kick. Theseus was young and strong, and helped by the magical string.

Prince Theseus: I'll grab the horns! I'll twist and twist! There!

Narrator 1: The Minotaur fell dead at his feet.

Prince Theseus: Now, where's the string? Is that it? No, it's a Minotaur tail. There, that must be it. Now to go back to the entrance.

Narrator 2: At the gate, Prince Theseus found Princess Ariadne waiting for him.

Princess Ariadne: I'll show you where to find other prisoners from your country.

Narrator 1: The other prisoners were freed. They rushed to the boat.

Princess Ariadne: Remember your promise, Prince Theseus. You must take me with you and make me your wife.

Prince Theseus: All right! Just hurry! I've got to get this sail up and get going.

Narrator 2: The black sail billowed in the wind as the young people made their escape.

Prince Theseus: As soon as we are safely away, I must change this sail for a white one.

Narrator 1: Princess Ariadne snuggled next to the prince and murmured.

Princess Ariadne: What joy it will be to be married to you!

Narrator 2: Prince Theseus remembered some very attractive girls in Athens. He really didn't feel ready to settle down, and Princess Ariadne seemed a bit pushy.

Prince Theseus: Well, uh, we'll talk about that later.

Narrator 1: On the way home, they stopped at an island for provisions. Prince Theseus sent Princess Ariadne to buy them. Then he sailed away without her.

Narrator 2: In his haste, he forgot to change the sails. His father, King Aegeus, was watching from the cliff when the ship with the black sails arrived back in Athens.

King Aegeus: My son! My son is dead!

Narrator 1: In his despair, he threw himself into the ocean and drowned.

Narrator 2: Ever since it has been called the Aegean Sea.

Name _____ Period _____ Date _____

Theseus and the Minotaur Storytelling Guide

Introduction:

_____

_____

_____

_____

The Details of the Story:

_____

_____

_____

_____

_____

_____

_____

_____

_____

Conclusion:

_____

_____

_____

_____

Storytelling Grading Standard

1. I practiced telling my story.

   1   **2**   **3**   **4**   **5**

   went over   knew it well
   it once

2. I told my story with expression to make it interesting and exciting.

   1   **2**   **3**   **4**   **5**

   kind of a   interesting
   monotone   and exciting

3. I used good pacing when I told my story.

   1   **2**   **3**   **4**   **5**

   too fast or   just the
   too slow   right speed

4. I maintained eye contact with my audience.

   1   **2**   **3**   **4**   **5**

   stared at the   looked at the
   paper or my feet   audience

5. This was my best work and I was proud of my effort.

   1   **2**   **3**   **4**   **5**

   just barely   did my best
   pulled it off

Total points _____

Little Women

by Louisa May Alcott, adapted by Chris Gustafson
NCTE Standard 2

Vocabulary Activities

Give each team of students a copy of the *"Little Women* Vocabulary" page. Ask students to cut apart the boxes, sort them into three or four groups, and give each group a title. Students explain to the rest of the class the reasons why they grouped their words as they did.

Vocabulary

burn and tear—Jo has apparently stood too close to the fire and part of her dress is singed; she has also ripped it.

elegant—stylish, fashionable

gloves—a big deal, no one can possibly go to a party without them

hot tongs—old-fashioned curling iron for curling hair

Marmee—what the girls call their mother

Miss March and Miss Josephine—the oldest daughter in a family was called "Miss" followed by the family last name, younger daughters were called "Miss" followed by their first names.

ought—should

parlor—a sort of extra living room

poplin—a kind of fabric, not very fancy

ringlets—hair curled into a kind of tube

scorched bundles—burned pieces

silk—a thin, special occasion fabric

soiled—dirty

spoilt—spoiled

Before Reading

The desire to look good for a special occasion transcends history and culture. Ask students to think carefully about what they chose to wear today, and why they chose what they did. Then have students write a description of what they would wear to a party given by some

78

friends if they knew someone they really wanted to impress would be there. Money is no object! Include as many details as possible about each item of clothing. Have students evaluate their description using the "Looking Good" grading standard.

Perform *Little Women*

Introduction

Marmee is raising her four daughters in genteel poverty and tries to communicate values to her children that are somewhat counter to the consumer- and appearance-oriented preoccupations of many of their friends. Meg, the oldest, is frustrated by the limits placed on her ability to dress as well as her peer group and is anxious to have a broader social life. Her younger sister, Jo, finds the demands of propriety annoying and would prefer to ignore them. The youngest sister, Beth, serves as comforter and fashion advisor in this play. Amy is mentioned but does not speak in this piece.

Cast of Characters

> *Narrator 1*
> *Narrator 2*
> *Meg—older sister, anxious, wants to look her best*
> *Jo—next oldest, tomboy, not obsessed by clothes*
> *Beth—helpful, comforting*

After Reading

Have students complete the "Problems and Solutions" page. The first part of the page includes events from the Reader's Theatre script. The last part asks students to predict other problems the characters might encounter at the party.

Additional Details

Meg and Jo manage to attend the party and make the best of their cobbled-together outfits. Each of the four girls responds in different ways to the broadening of their world as the older two "enter society." This is much more a book of relationships than a piece of historical fiction.

Alcott, Louisa May, *Little Women*. Scholastic, 248 pp.

Little Women Vocabulary

burn and tear	**elegant**	**gloves**
hot tongs	**Marmee**	**Miss March**
Miss Josephine	**ought**	**parlor**
poplin	**silk**	**scorched bundles**
soiled	**spoilt**	**ringlets**

Name _____ Period _____ Date _____

Looking Good

You've been invited to a party at a friend's house, and someone you want to impress is going to be there. Write two paragraphs describing what you would wear if money were no object. Be sure to include the color, the texture, and the style of your choices. Don't forget shoes!

_____

_____

_____

_____

_____

_____

_____

_____

_____

_____

_____

_____

_____

_____

_____

_____

Name _____ Period _____ Date _____

Looking Good Grading Standard

1. My description includes two well-written paragraphs.

   1   **2**   **3**   **4**   **5**

   complete sentences   good paragraph
   are a mystery   form

2. I included details about the color and style of my clothing.

   1   **2**   **3**   **4**   **5**

   not many   lots of detail

3. I described a complete outfit.

   1   **2**   **3**   **4**   **5**

   whoops, forgot   it's all there
   vital parts

4. This was my best work and I was proud of my effort.

   1   **2**   **3**   **4**   **5**

   just tossed   did my best
   it together

Total points _____

Little Women

by Louisa May Alcott, adapted by Chris Gustafson
NCTE Standard 2

Meg: Jo, Jo, where are you?

Jo: Here.

Narrator 1: Jo was curled up by the window, eating apples and crying over a book.

Meg: Such fun! It's a note of invitation from Mrs. Gardiner for tomorrow night!

Narrator 2: Meg read the invitation.

Meg: Mrs. Gardiner would be happy to see Miss March and Miss Josephine at a little dance on New Year's Eve. Marmee is willing we should go. Now what shall we wear?

Jo: What's the use of asking that, when you know we shall wear our poplins, because we haven't got anything else.

Meg: If only I had silk! Mother says I may when I'm eighteen, but two years is an everlasting time to wait.

Jo: Your dress is as good as new, but I forgot the burn and tear in mine.

Meg: You must sit all you can and keep your back out of sight; the front is all right. My gloves will do, though they're not as nice as I'd like.

Jo: Mine are spoilt with lemonade, and I can't get any new ones, so I shall have to go without them.

Meg: You must have gloves, or I won't go! Gloves are more important than anything else, and you can't dance without them. Can't you fix them?

Jo: I'll hold them crunched up in my hand, then no one will know they're stained. Or, I'll tell you how we can manage. We'll each wear one good one and carry a bad one.

Meg: Your hands are bigger than mine; you'll stretch my glove.

Jo: Then I'll go without. I don't care what people say.

Narrator 1: Jo picked up her book and started to read again.

Meg: You may have it! Only don't stain it, and do behave nicely.

Narrator 2: On New Year's Eve, Meg and Jo were in the parlor, getting ready for the party.

Narrator 1: Beth and Amy, their younger sisters, were watching and helping.

Narrator 2: Meg wanted a few curls around her face. Jo tried to make them with a pair of hot tongs.

Beth: Ought they to smoke like that?

Jo: It's the dampness drying.

Beth: What a smell! It's like burnt feathers!

Jo: I'll take off the papers and you'll see a little cloud of ringlets.

Narrator 1: Jo took off the papers, but no cloud of ringlets appeared.

Narrator 2: The hair came with the papers, and the horrified Jo lay a row of little scorched bundles on the bureau in front of Meg.

Meg: Oh, oh, oh! What have you done? I'm spoilt! I can't go! My hair, my hair!

Jo: Just my luck! You shouldn't have asked me to do it. I always spoil everything. I'm no end sorry, but the tongs were too hot.

Beth: It isn't spoilt. Just tie your ribbons so the ends come on your forehead a bit, and it will look like the latest fashion. I've seen lots of girls do it so.

Meg: Serves me right for trying to be fine. I wish I'd let my hair alone!

Beth: It will soon grow out again.

Narrator 1: They looked good in their silver dresses. Each put on one nice glove and carried one soiled one.

Narrator 2: Meg's high-heeled slippers were dreadfully tight, and Jo's nineteen hairpins all seemed stuck straight into her head, but the girls would be elegant or die.

Little Women Problems and Solutions

In the *Little Women* Reader's Theatre, find the problems to the solutions that are listed. Then imagine what might happen to Meg and Jo at the party. Write two problems they might face there and a possible solution for each of those problems.

1. **Problem:** _____

   Solution: Jo will sit as much as possible and keep her back out of sight.

2. **Problem:** _____

   Solution: Meg and Jo will each wear one glove and carry one glove.

3. **Problem:** _____

   Solution: Beth ties ribbons so they fall on Meg's forehead.

4. **Problem:** _____

   Solution: Meg and Jo go to the party feeling uncomfortable.

Imagine what might happen to Meg and Jo at the party.

1. **Problem:** _____

   Solution: _____

2. **Problem:** _____

   Solution: _____

85

Ear Wax Germs

by Chris Gustafson
NCTE Standard 3

Vocabulary Activities

The vocabulary page asks students to read new vocabulary words and then analyze three words or phrases. Two of the words or phrases relate to the meaning of the vocabulary word; one does not. Students will cross out the word or phrase that does not relate, then write a brief explanation of why the remaining words go together.

Vocabulary Words

ear wax—a thick sort of build-up that accumulates in ears

germs—microscopic organisms that cause disease

infection—disease growing in a host

scene—a short section of a longer piece of writing

skimmed—read quickly

Before Reading

Make an overhead of the graphic organizer and work as a class to list all the types of book reports or book responses students can recall. Or have students do this activity individually or in groups.

Perform *Ear Wax Germs*

Cast of Characters

Narrator 1
Narrator 2
Joslyn—careful, a bit of a worrier
Omar—artistic, likes to tease

After Reading

Students will write their own Puppet Theatre play in response to a story or a scene from a book that they have read, and will use the "Puppet Theatre Grading Standard" for evaluation.

In this play, the class is reading and responding to Mildred D. Taylor's *The Land*, a Coretta Scott King award-winning book.

Taylor, Mildred D. *The Land*, Penguin Putnam Inc., 2001, 375 pp.

86

Ear Wax Germs Vocabulary

Cross out the word or phrase that does not relate to the vocabulary word. Explain how the two remaining words or phrases relate to each other.

1. **ear wax**   belly button lint   toe jam   blood

   _____

2. **scene**   short section   a part   a play

   _____

3. **skimmed**   thought about   on the surface   read quickly

   _____

4. **infection**   bacteria   swelling   viral

   _____

5. **germs**   infection   catching   illness

   _____

Ear Wax Germs

by Chris Gustafson
NCTE Standard 3

Narrator 1: Ms. Levine's class had divided into teams to work on their book responses. Omar and Joslyn were working together.

Narrator 2: They were supposed to pick a scene from the book they'd both just finished reading, rewrite it as a play, and perform it for the class using puppets made from paper and Popsicle sticks.

Narrator 1: Omar stuck a Popsicle stick in his ear.

Joslyn: Omar! Stop it! I'm not going to touch that if it's got all your ear wax germs on it.

Omar: Who says you have to touch it? I'm the artist for this team. I'll touch it. My ear wax germs don't bother me. Besides, there's no such thing as ear wax germs.

Joslyn: I'll *have* to touch it. Our play has more than two characters in it. We'll both have to move the puppets from behind the stage, and we'll both have to do more than one part. You draw the characters on construction paper and glue each one to a stick. I'll write the script.

Omar: The stage? Don't you mean two desks pushed together?

Joslyn: Whatever. Just get to work. You need to make four boys. Two are in their teens and two are younger.

Omar: What scene are we doing?

Joslyn: Where Paul-Edward takes his brothers and goes to fight with Mitchell.

Omar: So I should make five.

Joslyn: Five?

Omar: I remember Paul-Edward took along his two older brothers to fight Mitchell and his brother Robert, who was about Paul-Edward's age. That's five.

Joslyn: I'm leaving Robert out. He's not really important in the scene and we don't have enough hands for five characters.

Omar: Can you do that?

Joslyn: Sure. It will still make sense.

Narrator 2: Omar sketched quickly. He cut out two tall shapes and began to shade in their features with colored pencil.

Narrator 1: Joslyn frowned over her paper. She wrote, crossed out, erased, and wrote some more.

Narrator 2: Omar poked Joslyn's arm.

Omar: See? Here are the older brothers.

Narrator 1: Omar had drawn brown pants on the two tall puppets. One wore a white shirt and one wore a red shirt.

Narrator 2: The shirts had long sleeves and no collars. They looked old-fashioned.

Joslyn: Good. The clothes look just right. But the faces are wrong.

Omar: What?

Narrator 1: Omar had colored each face a rich, dark brown.

Joslyn: That's the wrong color for Hammond and George.

Omar: How come?

Narrator 2: He pointed to the cover of the book. Two African American boys stood holding axes. Their clothes looked like the ones Omar had drawn.

Narrator 1: Joslyn opened the book to the first chapter.

Joslyn: Remember? Paul-Edward was a slave, and his mom was a slave, but his dad was the slave owner. Hammond and George were really half-brothers and they were white.

Narrator 2: Omar complained.

Omar: It's a long book, and that part was right at the front.

Joslyn: That's a really important part. It matters during the whole book.

Narrator 1: Omar hunted through his backpack and pulled out an eraser.

Omar: I'll fix it.

Narrator 2: Joslyn kept writing. Omar finished the two older boys and went to work on the two younger ones.

Omar: Okay, I don't want to do any more erasing. Mitchell and Paul-Edward were African American, right?

Narrator 1: Joslyn pushed the book over to Omar.

Joslyn: I'm busy. You check.

Narrator 2: Omar skimmed quickly through the first chapter. Then he went back to his drawings. Soon he was gluing the characters to their Popsicle sticks.

Omar: Okay. I'm done.

Narrator 1: Joslyn set her pen down and looked at the puppets.

Joslyn: That's super!

Omar: Mitchell is darker than Paul-Edward because his parents were both slaves. Paul-Edward looks like he's sort of in the middle.

Narrator 2: Omar and Joslyn ducked behind their desks to practice. Joslyn taped the pages of the script to the side of the desks so they could read their lines while they moved their characters.

Omar: Your writing is really hard to read.

Joslyn: Stop complaining. I'll type it in a big font before we have to perform.

Narrator 1: Omar handed Joslyn the two smaller puppets.

Narrator 2: He kept the two taller ones.

Joslyn: Wait a minute! Which puppet has the ear wax germs?

Narrator 1: Omar just smiled.

Omar: I guess I lost track. I'm not really sure.

Narrator 2: Joslyn wrinkled her nose. She picked up the two smaller puppets by their sticks.

Omar: Don't be stupid. There's no such thing as ear wax germs.

Joslyn: Maybe not. but if I get an ear infection from your puppets, you'll have to do the play all by yourself.

Narrator 1: Omar thought for just a few seconds. Then he took the shorter puppets from Joslyn and handed her the taller ones.

Puppet Theatre Grading Standard

Choose a scene from your book that involves at least two but no more than four characters. Write at least one page of dialogue (conversation) between the characters showing the audience something about the conflict in the book and showing what the characters are like. Make at least two Popsicle stick puppets. Rehearse the scene using your puppets. You will perform your scene in front of the class.

1. I have written a scene from my book that is at least one page long.

1	**2**	**3**	**4**	**5**
fewer, lame paragraphs				more than one page

2. My scene shows a conflict in the book.

1	**2**	**3**	**4**	**5**
not clear about conflict				it's clear

3. My scene shows what my characters are like.

1	**2**	**3**	**4**	**5**
they could be just anyone				shows character traits

4. My puppets are carefully done.

1	**2**	**3**	**4**	**5**
just threw them together				time and effort shows

5. I practiced my puppet scene—it was easy to hear and I was familiar with the lines.

1	**2**	**3**	**4**	**5**
just read the whole thing				I knew the scene

6. I put a lot of effort into my scene and it's my best work.

1	**2**	**3**	**4**	**5**
hmmm . . .				my best

Total points _____

Revision Group Goes Skateboarding

by Chris Gustafson
NCTE Standards 4, 5, 6

Vocabulary

List the vocabulary words and phrases on the board, divide students into groups of four, and introduce vocabulary skits. Adjust the number of words and phrases to match your class, copy as many vocabulary pages as you need, and hand each group the directions for the skits with their vocabulary word or phrase written in the blank spot. They will act out a short scene that shows the meaning of their vocabulary word or phrase, during which the word or phrase itself may not be used. Each member of the group must act and speak during the skit. At the conclusion of each skit, the class will guess which word or phrase was being depicted. It may be helpful to set a few group rules for classroom drama. For example, there should be no physical contact between group members. Do not depict scenes that violate school codes for violent or inappropriate behavior. Those people you see on the screen are *acting*—that's not real blood—so what you show doesn't really have to be happening.

Vocabulary Words

dialogue—conversation

dingy—dirty and run down

five senses—hearing, sight, taste, touch, smell

graphic—explicit

paragraph—a related group of sentences

piece—short writing selection

quotation marks—punctuation to denote conversation in writing

revision—to change something in order to improve it

symbols—marks that stand for something else

Before Reading

Draw a small circle within a large circle on the board or an overhead. In the smaller center circle, write the phrase "revising writing." Ask students to brainstorm all the words they can think of that relate to this concept. Then pass out the taxonomy sheet and have students transfer their revision words and phrases to the alphabetical list, along with any other ideas that come to mind as they are creating the lists.

Perform *Revision Group Goes Skateboarding*

Cast of Characters

> Narrator 1
> Narrator 2
> LaShonda— won't let Joey off the hook
> Mai—serious, critical
> Joey—lazy, impatient

After Reading

Have students create a grading standard for two paragraphs describing themselves doing a physical activity that they enjoy. Use the taxonomy to create the elements for the grading standard. Students will write their paragraphs, then use the grading standard they created to evaluate their writing, meet in revision groups to share their work, and revise their first drafts.

Name _____ Period _____ Date _____

Revision Group Goes Skateboarding Vocabulary

With your group, think of a short scene that would *show* (not tell) the meaning of the vocabulary word or phrase you've been assigned. Everyone in the group must have an acting and a speaking part. Do not touch other cast members, say aloud the word or phrase you are acting out, or violate any school rules in your skit. Use a dictionary if no one in your group knows the meaning of the word or phrase you've been assigned.

Your word or phrase is:

_____

Name _____ Period _____ Date _____

Revision Group Goes Skateboarding Vocabulary

With your group, think of a short scene that would *show* (not tell) the meaning of the vocabulary word or phrase you've been assigned. Everyone in the group must have an acting and a speaking part. Do not touch other cast members, say aloud the word or phrase you are acting out, or violate any school rules in your skit. Use a dictionary if no one in your group knows the meaning of the word or phrase you've been assigned.

Your word or phrase is:

_____

Name _____ Period _____ Date _____

Revision Group Goes Skateboarding Vocabulary

With your group, think of a short scene that would *show* (not tell) the meaning of the vocabulary word or phrase you've been assigned. Everyone in the group must have an acting and a speaking part. Do not touch other cast members, say aloud the word or phrase you are acting out, or violate any school rules in your skit. Use a dictionary if no one in your group knows the meaning of the word or phrase you've been assigned.

Your word or phrase is:

_____

Revision Group Goes Skateboarding Taxonomy

A _____

_____

B _____

_____

C _____

_____

D _____

_____

E _____

_____

F _____

_____

G _____

_____

H _____

_____

I _____

_____

J _____

_____

K _____

_____

L _____

_____

M _____

_____

N _____

_____

O _____

_____

P _____

_____

Q _____

R _____

S _____

T _____

U _____

V _____

W _____

X _____

Y _____

Z _____

Revision Group Goes Skateboarding

by Chris Gustafson
NCTE Standards 4, 5, 6

Narrator 1: LaShonda, Mai, and Joey pulled their desks into a circle.

Narrator 2: Their revision group was meeting, and it was Joey's turn to read a piece he'd written.

Joey: I don't get why I have to read this in revision group. It's done! See?

Narrator 1: Joey pointed to the bottom of his word-processed page.

Narrator 2: The words "THE END" were printed in capital letters.

Mai: Just because you wrote "THE END" does not mean it's finished.

LaShonda: Don't be stupid, Joey.

Narrator 1: Mai looked up at the overhead screen. Their teacher had written a large number five.

Mai: The first reading is for the five senses.

LaShonda: Read it aloud, Joey.

Narrator 1: Joey began to read his piece aloud.

Narrator 2: It was about the first time he went to a skateboard park.

Mai: Stop!

Joey: What? What's wrong?

LaShonda: What did the skateboard park look like?

Mai: Yeah, did it have a fence around it? Was there someone collecting money?

Joey: Nah, it was free.

LaShonda: Some of those free ones are really dingy.

Joey: No, this one was in good shape.

Mai: Keep reading.

Narrator 1: Joey told about his first run.

Narrator 2: He crashed.

LaShonda: How did that feel?

Joey: How do you think it felt? It hurt and I looked stupid.

Mai: Put that in.

Narrator 1: Joey wrote a note on his paper.

Narrator 2: He kept reading.

LaShonda: Was it really noisy?

Joey: No, there were only a few people there.

Mai: The skateboard wheels on the ramp make a cool sound. You should put that in.

Joey: OK, now listen to the next part, that's where I did my first 180 ollie without crashing.

Narrator 1: Joey read a whole paragraph without LaShonda and Mai interrupting.

Narrator 2: Joey finished reading and grinned.

Joey: Pretty good, huh?

LaShonda: How did it smell, Joey? You're supposed to use all five senses.

Joey: How did you think I smelled? I stank. I got really sweaty.

LaShonda: Put it in! Make the reader think about that smell!

Narrator 1: Joey made gagging noises.

Narrator 2: Mai was checking off the five senses.

Mai: Did you taste anything?

Narrator 1: Joey thought for a moment.

Joey: Uh, I had a package of ranch flavored corn nuts. When I fell and bit my lip, it tasted . . .

LaShonda: Ooo! Leave that part out!

Narrator 2: The teacher drew a pair of lips on the overhead.

Mai: Okay, dialogue.

Narrator 1: LaShonda grabbed Joey's paper and looked at it.

LaShonda: What is this, a quotation mark free zone? There's no dialogue.

Joey: Nobody talks!

Mai: Didn't you say anything?

Joey: Sure. But I'd get in trouble for putting it in a paper for school. Those crashes really hurt.

LaShonda: So be a little less graphic.

Joey: Like, "Oh, sugar?" I don't think so!

Mai: Or, you know, put all those little symbols in quotes like they do in the comics. That would be funny, and true too.

LaShonda: Every time you crashed, you could make the line of symbols a little longer.

Mai: Then at the end, when you go home, you should have your mom ask you how it went.

Joey: And I'll just say, "fine."

Narrator 2: The teacher wrote on the overhead, "Time's up."

Narrator 1: Joey looked at his paper. It was covered with notes and arrows.

Joey: Thanks so much, you two. I was done when I got here. Now I have all this work to do.

LaShonda: Oh, stop whining. You know you have it on disk. It won't take long to fix it.

Mai: Plus it's way better now. You owe us big time.

Joey: Well, OK. Thanks I guess. Just you wait, LaShonda. It's your turn for revision group tomorrow.

Name _____ Period _____ Date _____

Grading Standard for _____ Goes _____ Paragraphs

1. My description includes two well-written paragraphs.

   1   **2**   **3**   **4**   **5**

   complete sentences   good paragraph
   are a mystery

2.

3.

4.

5.

6. This piece is my best work and I'm proud of it.

   1   **2**   **3**   **4**   **5**

   not much effort   I did my best

Total points _____

99

_____ Goes _____

Fill your name in the first blank and the name of an activity you like to do in the second blank, for example, Juan Goes Rockclimbing. Write two paragraphs describing yourself doing the activity you chose. Evaluate your paragraphs using the grading standard you helped to create.

_____

_____

_____

_____

_____

_____

_____

_____

_____

_____

_____

_____

Advice for First-Time Travelers

by Chris Gustafson
NCTE Standards 7, 8

Vocabulary Activities

Students will work individually or in groups to fill out the example/description/comparison chart of vocabulary words for this selection.

Vocabulary Words

animation—making still drawings look like they are moving

anti-war demonstrators—people who rallied to get U.S. troops out of Vietnam

civil rights marches—parades of protesters demanding equal rights for African Americans in the 1950s and 1960s

fuel efficiency—using less fuel

jet lag—disorientation after flying through different time zones

microfiche—an elderly technology that stores a lot of print information on a small piece of film, readable through a special machine

tortillas—flat, round, bread-like food made of corn or wheat

Before Reading

Ask students to think of a time they went on a trip, remember three important things they packed to take along, and share what they took with a partner. Brainstorm individually, in groups, or as a class what would be important to pack when traveling. Besides what to pack, what are some other travel tips?

Perform *Advice for First-Time Travelers*

Cast of Characters

> Narrator 1
> Narrator 2
> Christina—a bit spacey, puts things off
> Jayson—enthusiastic, plans ahead
> Thomas—creative, thorough

After Reading

Have each student choose a travel destination and list seven travel tips for their proposed trip. Teach students to make a fold-and-cut book. Students will write and illustrate their tips in the book.

Name _____ Period _____ Date _____

Advice for First-Time Travelers Vocabulary

Fill in each box. Give an example of, description of, and comparison for, each word.

	Example	Description	Comparison
animation	"The Simpsons," any cartoon show	A series of still drawings arranged so the art seems to move.	Animation is to cartoons as acting is to theatre.
antiwar demonstrators			
civil rights marches			
fuel efficiency			
jet lag			
microfiche			
tortillas			

What to Pack?

Travel Tips

Advice for First-Time Travelers

by Chris Gustafson
NCTE Standards 7, 8

Narrator 1: Christina, Jason, and Thomas pulled their chairs closer together.

Narrator 2: They had ten minutes to brainstorm ideas for their independent research projects.

Jayson: I've been thinking about doing this project since my sister had Ms. Bricklin two years ago. I already know what I want to do.

Thomas: You still have to help with the brainstorm. We have to turn in a list of ten ideas.

Jayson: Put mine down first. I want to write a history of our town during the 60s and early 70s. My dad says there were civil rights marches and antiwar demonstrations, but I never learned about them in school.

Thomas: Christina, how about you?

Christina: I have no idea what I want to do. This project is so huge! I can't think of anything I want to spend six weeks learning about.

Jayson: Come on, Christina. Think of an idea for our list.

Narrator 1: Christina poked at the corner of a copy of *Seventeen* that was sticking out of her binder.

Christina: Oh, all right. Fashion photography.

Jayson: Write down "Japanese pottery." And "international desserts."

Thomas: How about women in sports? Or how computer animation works? Or how to scuba dive?

Jayson: My sister did hers on earthquakes in our state and had a big plan for how the whole city could be more prepared. Her best friend wrote a play about raising chickens.

Thomas: Just one more idea. Come on, Christina. We've got to write something down.

Christina: Tortillas.

Jayson: Tortillas?

Narrator 2: The bell rang. Thomas wrote "tortillas" at the bottom of their list and handed it to Ms. Bricklin on the way out the door.

Narrator 1: The next week Ms. Bricklin's class met in the library to start their research. Christina, Thomas, and Jayson were in the same computer cluster.

Jayson: All right! The newspaper Web site looks good. They must have old articles on civil rights. What did you decide on for your project, Thomas?

Thomas: I'm researching the history of car design, especially fuel efficiency and safety. Then I'm going to build my own model of a car for the future.

Narrator 2: Thomas scrolled through some choices on the school library catalog.

Thomas: There's a couple of books that might help. I'll have to go to the public library, too.

Jayson: Christina, what are you doing?

Christina: A list.

Joey: Your independent project is a list?

Christina: My life is a list. The Spanish Club trip to Mexico leaves next week. I'm figuring out what to pack.

Jayson: You're going to Mexico? Everyone on the Mexico trip was supposed to get started on the project a week early so they wouldn't get behind while they were gone.

Christina: I can't even think about the project. I can't think about anything but the trip. Leave me alone!

Narrator 1: Jayson went back to reading his Web site. Thomas located the books on car design and settled down at a table to take notes.

Jayson: The earliest articles on this Web site are from 1990! I'm going to have to go to the downtown library and look on microfiche. That's so lame.

Thomas: Don't complain. You have to have a bunch of different kinds of sources for the project. Maybe you can find someone local to interview, too.

Jayson: Good idea.

Christina: Quiet, you two. I'm planning my packing!

Narrator 2: During the time the Spanish Club was gone, Ms. Bricklin's class made several more visits to the library. Thomas spent Saturday afternoon interviewing car mechanics. Jayson found a film on the local anti-Vietnam War protests at the public library.

Narrator 1: The Spanish Club got back into town on a Monday. Christina made it back to school on Wednesday. She had her head down on her desk in Ms. Bricklin's class.

Thomas: Hey, Christina! How was your trip?

Narrator 2: Christina kept her head down. Her voice was muffled.

Christina: Not so loud. Jet lag gives me a headache.

Thomas: You still have jet lag?

Christina: Some people get it worse than others. I'm exhausted.

Thomas: You stayed out late a lot in Mexico?

Christina: Well, sometimes. But I wasn't very careful about what I ate, so I got really sick.

Narrator 1: Christina lifted up her head and looked at Thomas and Jayson.

Jayson: Wow!

Thomas: Definitely a no-sunscreen victim.

Narrator 2: Burned patches were peeling off Christina's forehead and one cheek.

Thomas: So, did you have a chance to think about your project?

Narrator 1: Christina groaned.

Christina: All I thought about was what not to do on a trip abroad. I think I made every possible mistake. I packed too much! My shoes gave me blisters! I forgot my diarrhea medicine!

Jayson: Actually, that's a pretty good project.

Christina: What is?

Jayson: What you learned about what not to do. The French Club is going on their trip after school is out. Why don't you make a booklet about what not to do when you travel abroad for them?

Thomas: Yeah, with lots of pictures. You could interview the other kids on your trip. Maybe some grown-ups who travel a lot. You couldn't have been the only one who . . .

Christina: . . . ever did something stupid on a trip? Well, there was Samantha getting in a car with that boy she'd just met and not telling her host mother. I guess a booklet is a pretty good idea.

Narrator 2: Christina started to smile, but moving her mouth made her sunburn sting.

Jayson: You were doing research all week, and you didn't even know it!

Name _____ Period _____ Date _____

Travel Tips Grading Standard

1. I have a title page with my name as the author.

   no _____ **0 points**   yes _____ **2 points**

2. I have seven pages of travel tips.

1	**2**	**3**	**4**	**5**	**6**	**7**
not quite						all there

3. My travel tips are interesting and useful.

1	**2**	**3**	**4**	**5**
boring and useless				interesting and useful

4. Each page is neatly illustrated.

1	**2**	**3**	**4**	**5**
sloppy and sparse				neat and well arranged

5. The illustrations help the reader understand the travel tips.

1	**2**	**3**	**4**	**5**
hard to tell they're related				they relate to the tips

6. The Travel Tips book is my best work and I'm proud of it.

1	**2**	**3**	**4**	**5**
not much time and effort				did my best

Total points _____

Sojourner Truth (born Isabella Baumfree)

by Chris Gustafson
NCTE Standard 9

Sojourner Truth was a powerful voice for the abolition of slavery and the rights of women during the 1800s in the United States.

Vocabulary Activities

On the vocabulary page, students will draw a cartoon illustrating the meaning of each of the vocabulary words.

Vocabulary Words

abolitionists—a political group opposed to slavery

head—get ahead of

Quaker—a religious group opposed to slavery

sojourner—a person who stays for a brief period of time during a journey

"Where did Christ come from?"—Sojourner Truth's audience would have been familiar with this phrase referring to the Biblical account of the birth of Christ as a result of the union of the Holy Spirit with Mary.

Before Reading

Individually, in groups, or as a class, have students complete the first two sections of the KWL chart about slavery. Since this age group is likely to answer the question, "What do you want to know?" with a resounding "Nothing," try using the phrase "What do you wonder?" for the middle part of the chart.

Perform *Sojourner Truth*

Cast of Characters

 Mau Mau Bett, Sojourner Truth's mother—loving, grieving, resigned
 John Dumont—thinks he is fair-minded
 Sojourner Truth—bold, eager to learn, determined

After Reading

Fill in the final section of the KWL chart. Teach students the three-level questioning strategy—how to look for information that is right there, for which they have to think and search, and for more open-ended questions when they are on their own. Students will apply the strategy using the "Three-Level Questions" sheet.

Krass, Peter, *Sojourner Truth, Antislavery Activist*, Chelsea House Publishers, 1998, 105 pp.

McKissack, Patricia C. and Frederick, *Sojourner Truth, Ain't I a Woman?* Scholastic,
 1992, 186 pp.

Sojourner Truth Vocabulary

Draw a cartoon in each of the boxes below to illustrate the vocabulary words

abolitionist	**Quaker**
sojourner	**slave**

Name _____ Period _____ Date _____

KWL/Slavery

What I Know About Slavery	What I Wonder About Slavery	What I Learned About Slavery

Sojourner Truth (born Isabella Baumfree)

by Chris Gustafson
NCTE Standard 9

Mau Mau Bett, Sojourner Truth's Mother: With my husband James, I raised up the children the best I could. I told 'em: Do what you're told. Always obey. Remember, there is a God who loves you. But it was hard, so hard. My older children, all sold away. They don't know where I be, and I don't know where they be. I can still hear Michael and Nancy screaming as they were taken. Our last Master wasn't so bad. When he died, my husband and I were freed. But what could we do? James was sick and could not work. We had no place to live, no jobs we could do. Since our first owners were Dutch, we barely spoke any English. We were allowed to live in the basement of the new owners as long as we worked for them. But our Peter and our Belle were sold away.

John Dumont, Belle's Owner: Belle was thirteen when I bought her. My wife didn't like her much, but Belle was strong and worked hard. When Belle wanted to marry Robert, and Robert's owner said no, I had to agree. Slaves from the same owner ought to marry, so their children will belong to that owner. Another woman was found for Robert, and I found Tom for Belle. Belle worked hard for me for fifteen years. There had been a change in the law, and I told her if she worked one more year for me, I would give her her freedom. The next year was bad for our crops, and Belle had hurt her hand. She couldn't work as hard as she had before. So I told her she would have to stay another year. Can you believe it? Belle just up and left. She walked out the door. She left Tom and their children. She decided she was free.

Belle at Forty-Six Years Old: My children were grown and gone. When I was praying, I heard a message from God telling me to go east. I quit my job as a housekeeper and walked away from New York. The next evening I met a Quaker woman at a farm where I'd stopped for some water. The woman asked me my name, and I told her it was Sojourner, a word that means traveler. For my last name, I picked Truth. Just like in the Bible, I want to walk in the light of God's truth.

Sojourner Truth: I took up with some abolitionists, and I went from meeting to meeting. I told them what it was like to be a slave, and I told them that women were just as good as men. Once I was speaking and a man began to complain and say that women were the weaker sex. He said women need to be helped into carriages and lifted over ditches and to have the best places everywhere. Nobody ever helps me into carriages, over mud puddles, or got me any best places. And ain't I a woman? Look at me! I have ploughed and I have planted. And I have gathered into barns. And no man could head me. And ain't I a woman? I have borne children and seen them sold into slavery, and when I cried out in a mother's grief, none heard me but Jesus. And ain't I a woman? You say Jesus was a man so that means God favors men over women. Where did your Christ come from? From God and a woman. Man had nothing to do with Him.

Three-Level Questions About *Sojourner Truth*

Answer each question in complete sentences on a separate piece of paper.

1. What happened to Sojourner Truth's brothers and sister? Sojourner was named Isabella when she was born, and nicknamed Belle. *(think and search)*

2. What was Sojourner Truth's mother's first language? *(think and search)*

3. What did John Dumont, Belle's owner, think of slaves getting married? *(right there)*

4. What did Belle do when Dumont broke his word about setting her free? *(right there)*

5. Choose a new name for yourself. Give at least two reasons to explain why you chose the name you did. *(on your own)*

6. Why do you think the abolitionists didn't want to hear Sojourner's message about women being just as good as men? *(on your own)*

7. How does the man who disagreed with Sojourner describe women? *(right there)*

8. In what ways has Sojourner's life not matched the description of how women should be treated? *(think and search)*

Rice Balls and Current Events

by Chris Gustafson
NCTE Standard 10

Vocabulary Activities

Students will work individually or in groups to fill in the squares on *"Rice Balls and Current Events* Vocabulary" page.

Vocabulary Words

cross-country—a long race run over open country

fluent—speaks quickly and easily

response—a reply or an answer

rice balls—cold cooked rice, often triangular-shaped, plain or filled

teriyaki—a flavoring used in some Japanese food

URL—Universal Resource Locator; what you type into the address box to get to a web site.

Before Reading

Students will work in groups using the graphic organizer to brainstorm what it is like to live in a different culture. They will share their ideas with the rest of the class.

Perform *Rice Balls and Current Events*

Cast of Characters

Narrator 1

Narrator 2

Miaki—athletic, willing to try new things

Chikako—girly, not quite as open to new things

After Reading

Assign half of the students to complete a character profile sheet on Miaki, the other half on Chikako. Pair students who have done different characters to use their character profiles to create a comparison chart on the two characters.

117

Name _____ Period _____ Date _____

Rice Balls and Current Events Vocabulary

Fill in each box.

Word or Phrase	What It Means	Example	Non-Example
rice balls	room-temperature seasoned rice, formed into triangles, often with a filling	rice balls with plum, rice balls with nori (seaweed)	a bowl of rice
teriyaki			
fluent			
URL			
cross-country			
response			

What It's Like to Live in a Different Culture

List ideas about what it's like to live in a different culture inside the circle. List the sources for your ideas outside the circle.

living in a different culture

Rice Balls and Current Events

by Chris Gustafson
NCTE Standard 10

Narrator 1: If Miaki and Chikako had gone to the same school in Japan, they would never have been friends. They just didn't have enough in common.

Miaki: Clothes! Chikako has gone crazy since there aren't school uniforms here. I don't think she wears the same outfit two times in the same month. Her fingernails have to match everything.

Chikako: I never met anyone who didn't care about how she looks. Miaki hardly wears any make-up. She probably only owns one lipstick.

Miaki: Chikako's not happy unless everyone is looking at her.

Chikako: How does Miaki expect anyone to notice her?

Miaki: Chikako acts like we were still in Japan. There's stuff we can do here that we couldn't do there, at least at my old school. Like the girl's cross-country team. Chikako doesn't want to try anything new.

Chikako: I'm trying new things all the time. Everything is new here! That doesn't mean it's right for me. I'm tired of new things.

Narrator 2: Out of 1400 students at their school, Miaki and Chikako were the only ones who had been born in Japan and spoke fluent Japanese as well as pretty good English. That was enough to make them friends.

Narrator 1: They liked to eat together at a lunchroom table by the windows.

Narrator 2: Miaki thumped her lunch tray on the table just as Chikako opened up her lunch bag.

Chikako: School lunch teriyaki chicken?

Miaki: It doesn't look so bad. You know I hate to make my own lunch.

Narrator 1: Chikako unwrapped three triangles of rice.

Narrator 2: Miaki pointed at one of them.

Chikako: Keep your hands off my rice balls!

Miaki: Cross-country tryouts make me hungry. Does that one have a sour plum in the center?

Chikako: None of your business.

Narrator 1: Chikako took a bite of the rice ball. Miaki could see the dark purple middle.

Miaki: Your mom makes great rice balls.

Narrator 2: Chikako finished off the rice ball.

Chikako: Enjoy your school lunch teriyaki!

Narrator 1: Miaki took a bite of the teriyaki. She made a face, but kept eating.

Miaki: Chikako, can you help me in the library after lunch?

Chikako: I guess. How come?

Miaki: I have to turn in my current event paper by the end of the day. I tried to read one last night, but after half an hour with my dictionary, I still didn't get it. And I can't keep going to cross-country tryouts if I have missing work.

Chikako: I don't see why you want to get so tired and hot and sweaty.

Narrator 2: Miaki giggled.

Chikako: What is it?

Miaki: I thought you could figure it out. There are girls AND boys on the team.

Chikako: Hot and smelly boys. Girls with runner's hair.

Narrator 1: After lunch, Chikako dragged Miaki to a free computer in the library.

Miaki: Why are we looking on the computer? I'm supposed to write about some news article.

Narrator 2: The internet connection was fast for once, and Chikako quickly typed in a URL.

Narrator 1: Chikako pointed to the Web site she had opened.

Chikako: There! Read the news article in Japanese. Write your paper in English.

Narrator 2: Both girls read the article about conflict in the Middle East quickly and easily.

Narrator 1: It took Miaki quite a bit longer to write her response to the article in English. She finished just before the bell.

Narrator 2: Chikako closed out a Web site she'd been looking at from a Japanese fashion magazine.

Miaki: Thanks, Chikako. I don't know why I didn't think of going to a Japanese news service.

Chikako: Want to come to my house after cross-country practice? If you help me make rice balls, you can have some for your lunch tomorrow.

Miaki: Practice is kind of late. Are you sure you want to wait?

Chikako: I can work in the library.

Miaki: Well, okay.

Narrator 1: Chikako studied a perfect blue nail.

Chikako: Maybe you could introduce me to some of those sweaty boys.

Character Sheet — Miaki or Chikako (circle your character)

Age: _____

Likes:

_____

_____

_____

Dislikes:

_____

_____

_____

Hopes:

_____

_____

_____

Fears:

_____

_____

_____

Other:

_____

_____

_____

Comparing Miaki and Chikako

Things that are only true of Miaki:

_____

_____

_____

_____

Things that are true of Miaki and Chikako:

_____

_____

_____

_____

Things that are only true of Chikako:

_____

_____

_____

_____

Class Newspaper

by Chris Gustafson
NCTE Standards 11, 12

Vocabulary Activities

Individually or in groups, have students research the three types of poetry mentioned in the play. Record their information on the vocabulary sheet.

Vocabulary Words

haikus—Japanese poetry with a set number of syllables per line
sonnets and cinquains—structured forms of poetry
standards—a description of goals to be met

Before Reading

Locate several copies of the local newspaper. Give a copy to each group of five or so students. Using the "Parts of a Newspaper" organizer, have them list the names of the newspaper sections and the types of articles in each section.

Perform *Class Newspaper*

Cast of Characters

Narrator 1
Narrator 2
Margaret—creative, a risk taker
Roneel—somewhat stubborn
Ms. Duong—flexible, creative
Bryan—opinionated

After Reading

Copy the "Types of Articles" page to suit the number of students in your class. Cut apart the boxes and have students draw the slips to determine what type of article they will produce. Use the grading standards to evaluate the articles.

125

Class Newspaper Vocabulary

Use print or internet sources to define the three kinds of poetry. Copy an example of each type (cite your source) or make up your own.

Haiku

Definition: _____

_____

Example: _____

_____

Sonnet

Definition: _____

_____

Example: _____

_____

Cinquain

Definition: _____

_____

Example: _____

_____

Name _____ Period _____ Date _____

Parts of a Newspaper

Sections	Types of Articles in the Section
	1. 2. 3. 4. 5.
	1. 2. 3. 4 5.
	1. 2. 3. 4. 5.
	1. 2. 3. 4. 5.
	1. 2. 3. 4. 5.
	1. 2. 3. 4. 5.

Class Newspaper

by Chris Gustafson
NCTE Standards 11 ,12

Narrator 1: Margaret was tired of writing five-paragraph essays in her language arts class.

Narrator 2: Margaret was tired of writing sonnets and haikus.

Narrator 1: She couldn't stand to write one more paragraph from the point of view of a character in a classic novel.

Narrator 2: She raised her hand.

Margaret: As long as we're meeting the standards or the six traits or the learning goals or whatever, what does it matter what we're writing? Let's do a class newspaper.

Roneel: The school already has a student newspaper. Why do we need another one?

Margaret: Because it would be ours! Can we, Ms. Duong?

Ms. Duong: A newspaper is a lot of work.

Margaret: It would be different from regular school work. We'd work hard because other kids would read what we wrote.

Bryan: The school paper never takes on the hard issues.

Margaret: Yeah, and all the athletes and the popular kids are in it, not regular people.

Roneel: What's wrong with sports? I want to read about athletes!

Ms. Duong: Okay, here's the deal. For the next two weeks I'll teach you newspaper writing. We'll see if we can meet the standards by doing it. Then we'll take a vote to see if we want to do a newspaper.

Narrator 1: Ms. Duong's class read the local newspapers. They listed the types of articles they found.

Narrator 2: They studied news articles and sports articles and feature stories. They studied editorials and reviews and cartoons.

Narrator 1: At the end of the two weeks, they decided to try it. Ms. Duong taped up six pieces of butcher paper around the room, one for each section of their paper.

Ms. Duong: Everyone take a pen and write as many story ideas as you can on each paper.

Margaret: I want to be a reporter at the next site council meeting.

Narrator 2: She wrote her story idea on the news poster. It was easy to tell Margaret's story ideas. On every poster, they were the ones written in thick green pen.

Narrator 1: Bryan was stuck by the editorial poster.

Bryan: Why have spirit weeks? Why do we have to test into honors classes? That's what I want to write about.

Roneel: I'm gonna review school lunches. Then I'm going to review the food at the sub shop across the street. Then that new science fiction movie at the multiplex.

Narrator 2: After the posters were full of ideas, Ms. Duong put up another chart.

Ms. Duong: OK—everyone sign up for an article. If all the spaces in sports are filled, for example, pick another kind of article.

Roneel: I only want to write about sports!

Margaret: Forget it, Roneel. Didn't you listen to Ms. Duong? Nobody can write the same kind of story ever week. Otherwise we don't all meet all the standards.

Roneel: You're going to be sorry when it's my week to draw the cartoon. It's going to be awful!

Narrator 1: The writers of each kind of story met by their posters.

Narrator 2: They picked ideas and an editor for each group. They wrote a grading standard for each type of story.

Margaret: Okay news group writers! I'm your editor! First drafts are due on Friday!

Narrator 1: On Friday the groups met again.

Bryan: Listen up, editorial group. Pull up a chair. We're all going to read our pieces aloud and fix the parts that don't work.

Narrator 2: Final drafts were due on Tuesday. Roneel printed his in the library during the passing period before class.

Roneel: Margaret, see my story on the girl's volleyball game. It was so excellent!

Narrator 1: Margaret gave the story a quick look.

Margaret: Ugh—typos! I'm not your editor.

Ms. Duong: On tasks, everyone! Everything needs to be perfect before we publish.

Bryan: I've read this story 'til I'm cross-eyed. I wouldn't see a mistake if it jumped off the page and bit me.

Narrator 2: At last the paper was done.

Ms. Duong: Sit down everyone. Take out your evaluation forms while I pass out your copies. Write down your comments as your read each article.

Margaret: All right.

Narrator 1: Everyone settled in to read. For the first time in weeks, it was completely quiet.

Name _____ Period _____ Date _____

Types of Articles

editorial	fashion feature	advice column	editorial cartoon	school news story
movie review	restaurant review	book review	city news story	national news story
international news story	sports news story	cartoon strip	interview	food feature
editorial	fashion feature	advice column	editorial cartoon	school news story
movie review	restaurant review	book review	city news story	national news story
international news story	sports news story	cartoon strip	interview	food feature

131

Name _____ Period _____ Date _____

News Story Grading Standard

1. Correct spelling, punctuation, and grammar are used.

   1   **2**   **3**   **4**   **5**

   pretty sloppy   all correct

2. The first sentence is interesting and makes the reader want to read more.

   1   **2**   **3**   **4**   **5**

   boring   interesting

3. My story is at least four paragraphs long with the most important information in the first paragraph.

   1   **2**   **3**   **4**   **5**

   short and   it is
   disorganized

4. My article tells who, what, when, where, why, and how.

   1   **2**   **3**   **4**   **5**

   leaves a   got them all
   few out

5. There's a picture or photo with my article.

   0   **3**

   no   yes

6. This article is my best work and I'm proud of it.

   1   **2**   **3**

   not much   did my best
   effort

Total points _____

Opinion/Editorial Grading Standard

1. Correct spelling, punctuation, and grammar are used.

   1   **2**   **3**   **4**   **5**

   pretty sloppy   all correct

2. The first sentence is interesting and makes the reader want to read more.

   1   **2**   **3**   **4**   **5**

   boring   interesting

3. My editorial is at least four paragraphs long with the most important
   information in the first paragraph.

   1   **2**   **3**   **4**   **5**

   short and   it is
   disorganized

4. My editorial states an opinion and includes many supporting details.

   1   **2**   **3**   **4**   **5**

   not too   rich with
   detailed   details

5. I've chosen an issue of interest to my audience.

   1   **2**   **3**

   maybe not   yes

6. This editorial is my best work and I'm proud of it.

   1   **2**   **3**   **4**   **5**

   not much   did my best
   effort

Total points _____

Name _____ Period _____ Date _____

Feature Story Grading Standard

1. Correct spelling, punctuation, and grammar are used.

   1　　　　　**2**　　　　　**3**　　　　　**4**　　　　　**5**

   pretty sloppy　　　　　　　　　　　　　　　　　　　all correct

2. The first sentence is interesting and makes the reader want to read more.

   1　　　　　**2**　　　　　**3**　　　　　**4**　　　　　**5**

   boring　　　　　　　　　　　　　　　　　　　　　interesting

3. My story is at least four paragraphs long with the most important information in the first paragraph.

   1　　　　　**2**　　　　　**3**　　　　　**4**　　　　　**5**

   short and　　　　　　　　　　　　　　　　　　　it is
   disorganized

4. My article tells at least ten pieces of information about my topic.

   1　　　　　**2**　　　　　**3**　　　　　**4**　　　　　**5**

   leaves the　　　　　　　　　　　　　　　　　　lots of info
   reader guessing

5. I chose interesting, lively words for my story.

   1　　　　　　　　　　　**2**　　　　　　　　　　　**3**

   no　　　　　　　　　　　　　　　　　　　　　　　yes

6. This article is my best work and I'm proud of it.

   1　　　　　**2**　　　　　**3**　　　　　**4**　　　　　**5**

   not much　　　　　　　　　　　　　　　　　　did my best
   effort

Total points _____

Name _____ Period _____ Date _____

Review Grading Standard

1. Correct spelling, punctuation, and grammar are used.

    1   **2**   **3**   **4**   **5**
    pretty sloppy   all correct

2. The first sentence is interesting and makes the reader want to read more.

    1   **2**   **3**   **4**   **5**
    boring   interesting

3. My story is at least four paragraphs long with the most important information in the first paragraph.

    1   **2**   **3**   **4**   **5**
    short and   it is
    disorganized

4. My article states an opinion and gives many supporting details.

    1   **2**   **3**   **4**   **5**
    not too   rich with
    detailed   details

5. My article has a reviewing standard.

    0   **3**
    no   yes

6. This article is my best work and I'm proud of it.

    1   **2**   **3**   **4**   **5**
    not much   did my best
    effort

Total points _____

Name _____ Period _____ Date _____

Comic Grading Standard

1. My comic has four to six panels.

1	**2**	**3**	**4**	**5**
didn't quite finish				four to six

2. There are speech bubbles and the words are spelled correctly.

1	**2**	**3**	**4**	**5**
spelling?				all correct

3. The comic takes an idea and follows through with it—there's a beginning, middle, and end.

1	**2**	**3**	**4**	**5**
disorganized				organized like a story

4. The panels are neatly drawn with a foreground and a background.

1	**2**	**3**	**4**	**5**
messy and poorly done				neat and well done

5. Each panel has a lot of detail.

1	**2**	**3**	**4**	**5**
not much				a lot

6. The comic is my best work and I'm proud of it.

1	**2**	**3**	**4**	**5**
not much effort				did my best

Total points _____

Name _____ Period _____ Date _____

Editorial Cartoon Grading Standard

1. My cartoon is the assigned size.

   1   **2**   **3**   **4**   **5**
   didn't fill my   just right
   space

2. There are captions or speech bubbles and the words are spelled correctly.

   1   **2**   **3**   **4**   **5**
   spelling?   all correct

3. My cartoon makes a clear point about a current issue.

   1   **2**   **3**   **4**   **5**
   kind of   clear and
   confusing   pointed

4. The cartoon is neatly drawn with a foreground and a background.

   1   **2**   **3**   **4**   **5**
   messy and   neat and
   poorly done   well done

5. The cartoon has a lot of detail.

   1   **2**   **3**   **4**   **5**
   not much   a lot

6. This cartoon is my best work and I'm proud of it.

   1   **2**   **3**
   not much   did my best
   effort

Total points _____

137

9 781586 830908